HARNESS IN THE PARLOUR

A Book of Early Canadian Fact and Folklore

by Audrey I. Armstrong

MUSSON BOOK COMPANY

Toronto

First published in 1974 by
Musson Book Company
30 Lesmill Road, Don Mills, Ontario

ISBN 0-7737-1005-1

Printed in Canada

Design/Peter Maher & Associates

Illustrations/J. Merle Smith

2 3 4 5 THB 79 78 77 76

Lovingly dedicated to my mother,
Martha Gamble Andrews

Contents

Preface

Life differed slightly in each community and province of early Canada, but the basic attitudes, customs, and practices of the pioneer people fitted into much the same pattern. This book is an attempt to recall that pattern, as it existed from the late eighteenth century on into the Depression era - an era when necessity forced many people to revert to pioneer techniques and philosophies. Research for such a book has naturally involved countless hours of reading, frequent discussions with old-timers, and many delightful evenings poring over old postcard and photograph albums, "receipt" books, and scrapbooks.

I have written this book mainly for children, who have not known the old way of life, and have never "flown" from the roof of the privy using burdock leaves as wings or hiked down a cowpath on a cool June morning and gladly eased their cold bare feet into a warm cowflap, oozing between the toes. But I have also written it for those young people interested in returning to the simpler mode of living and old-time security, and for my own generation, who were raised during the Depression and thus experienced many of the discomforts *and* the happiness of that older life-style. And last, but by no means least, I have written it for my parents' generation, as a gesture of respect and honour for the senior citizens of our country, from whom I have gleaned so much of my material. They will, I hope, read it - or have it read to them - with an occasional chuckle and perhaps an enthusiastic, "Now, yes ... do you mind *that!*"

I wish to extend grateful appreciation to my many friends and relatives in the historic counties of Carleton and Lanark in the Ottawa Valley, for information freely given, and to my friends in Maple, Ontario, for their enthusiasm and encouragement. The staff and visitors at Black Creek Pioneer Village, where I have worked for the last five years, have also shared facts and ideas with me, and through them I have felt a closer affinity with the past. Finally, my sincere thanks to my husband and daughters, who have not only aided and abetted me, but have endured my pioneer eccentricities - and the clacking of my midnight typewriter. A.I.A.

Introduction

Watching the young men, tanned and clean-shaven, tearing down the old machinery shed to make room for a modern, flat-roofed structure, I pictured bearded men of long ago, big muscled men with adze in gnarled hand. Great Uncle William, Thomas standing by with hewing axe, ready to hurrah the men to action at a given sign. Brawny neighbours, sturdy as the beams they came to raise. Lying by in readiness, kegs of flat, blunt nails peculiar to the time, and baskets of wooden pegs whittled by the golden light of tallow-dip the night before, when other work had ceased.

In the kitchen, full-skirted women, and the fragrance of home-baked berry pies fresh from the big black oven. Huge platters of salt pork, still spitting from the pan, home-made bread and biscuits, bowls of Irish cobblers, piping hot, spread upon the harvest table. The womenfolk bustling about, waiting for the men to stride in, two and three together, sweating, joking, as they drew water from the pump.

A moment of thanks for food, and wholesome fellowship, for day to work and night for needed rest. The men planning their work even as they ate, while the pungent smell of freshly hewn wood still reached their nostrils through the open kitchen door.

In those days, neighbours were really neighbours, I thought, prepared to travel long, slow miles to lend a helping hand. I watched as the dusty shingles, now weather-worn and green with moss, ripped through the rusted nails, baring oaken beams raised with sweat and toil a century before. The workers spoke: "Let's take five, and have a cigarette." Their cheerful voices drifted in through the picture window above the modern sink in the same old house, renovated, but built of sturdy logs by those pioneers and kindly neighbours, long since turned into the sod they'd arduously cleared so many years ago.

I sighed a little, brushed away a tear for days I'd never known. And I hoped one day to somehow preserve a small part of that earlier mode of living – in words, perhaps, not so easily demolished as a century-old building. "We'll take the truck," the voices said, "and clear up this mess before it's time to chore."

1

The Homestead

"Over the river and through the wood
To grandfather's house we go . . . "
- Lydia Marie Child

In much of eastern Canada before Confederation, grandfather's house was very often located over the river and back through the woods. And when grandfather was a boy, the house might well have been just a log cabin with its surrounding cluster of barns and sheds.

The first pathway to a pioneer homestead was a rough trail the settlers blazed by notching trees as they trekked. Later, an oxen sledge trail was cleared to the chosen site. Once a settling family chose a site for their homestead, they faced the laborious task of clearing the land for the buildings and the first harvest. They had little means of hauling materials to the site, so they converted whatever was available into a simple home. Consequently, many of the early cabins were constructed of three or four different kinds of wood - ash, elm, cedar, maple, perhaps oak for the beams and mantel-piece. In areas where stone was scarce, even the chimneys were made of hardwood, often with disastrous results.

Gradually, as the farm prospered and the family grew, an extension was added to the cabin, frequently larger than the original structure. Then the entire building might be covered with clapboard. A porch over the cellar entrance and a large verandah were sometimes added, and the whole house was usually painted. Contrary to popular belief, the pioneers painted their buildings and furniture as soon as possible. Some used ox-blood for the buildings; others mixed whisky or buttermilk (both were cheap and available) with ochre to protect and brighten the wood.

Everybody went straight into the kitchen upon entering the house in olden days. A motherly or wifely admonition to "wipe your feet" was the expected - if often disregarded - welcome into the kitchen's warmth. To prevent mud from being tramped in from the messy path leading to the house, housewives sometimes laid evergreen boughs outside the doorway. Bootscrapers were attached to the stoop for cleaning off mud or snow, and "boot-jacks" for removing the high Wellington boots were also gentle reminders to those entering the kitchen door. As a further precaution, wet sawdust was strewn over a muddy path, and during winter ashes were sprinkled over icy pathways to the house, barns, and privy.

The old homes were draughty. To keep out winter winds that swept along the floors, and rain that splashed in under the door, special draught boards were attached at an angle to the base of doors leading outside. Much of the draught could also be lessened by pushing semicircular rugs or even heavy coats or old quilts up against the base of the door. These were religiously shoved back into place each time someone entered or left the house. During a cold spell or blizzard, old quilts were often nailed over a north window as another effective deterrent. And, in the finer homes, draught bolsters (cloth-stuffed rolls) were placed on the floor against inside doors leading to closed-off, seldom used rooms such as the parlour or guest room.

Cold air also seeped in through the chinks between the logs of cabins, and in later years through the cracks in the walls of summer kitchens. Resourceful pioneers securely stuffed the cracks with strips of rags forced in between the logs or boards with the tip of an old knife. They cut strips of cotton from sugar bags (whenever these were available) to paste over the cracks, and then applied layers of newspaper with a boiled flour-and-water paste - surely the first wallpaper in Canada!

Later, as "store-boughten" wallpaper became less expensive, settlers pasted it over the layers of newspaper. Never was an old layer removed, for it proved to be good insulation in a draughty home. Wallpaper in those days was printed in squares to be cut and fitted to the required size, rather than in narrow rolls as we know it. The cheapest papers were usually in dull, unimaginative browns that did little to brighten the appearance of a room. They did freshen up the air in a smoke-permeated room, though, and perhaps their application served as a restorative to an often weary morale.

The old trap doors were aptly named. Many was the time a "poor unfortunate" tumbled cellarward, realizing too late that some family member had left the trap door open while storing fresh vegetables from the garden out back.

Often only a hole in the ground deep enough to hold root vegetables (and called, naturally enough, a root cellar) was to be found beneath the trap door. In some homes the cellar was dug out as large as the space under an entire room, and either a ladder or a flight of steep steps was extended down to its earthen floor. Here, crocks for butter, lard, and eggs were fitted into cool depressions in the ground, and pans of milk were set out.

In the finer, larger homes, full-sized basements with huge fireplaces for cooking were built. A family might live in such a basement until the upper stories were completed. Then a simple, rope-controlled elevator with shelves was sometimes installed in a pantry off the kitchen, for the convenient moving of supplies to and from the cool basement.

When pioneers spoke of a "lowering oven", they meant a brick oven in which a fire had been built, then gradually reduced to coals and scraped out, leaving only the hot bricks to provide heat for baking. The temperature in this oven had just one way to go and that was "lower". When stoves took the place of the open fire for cooking purposes, the same result could be achieved by simply "letting the fire out" and allowing the oven to gradually cool down.

As the cast-iron, wood-burning stoves came into existence, they were advertised as "new-fangled warming machines". They were much more practical than the fireplace for cooking, "threw off" more heat into the room, and even prevented the fragrance of "good things to eat" from escaping up the chimney as it often did with fireplace draughts.

The first stoves were built much lower than later models, to enable the cook to peer into the high and heavy cooking utensils left over from the days of fireplace cooking. Perhaps another reason was that the pioneers tended to be somewhat shorter than people today, as you may realize if you have ever bumped your head on the low doorway of a century-old home.

There were few ornaments in the pioneer home, but most families at least owned a chimney piece. Made of china and easily recognized by its unfinished flat back, the chimney piece was a very popular gift in the nineteenth century. Cheaper types were mass-produced, and were known as "fairings" because they were frequently handed out as prizes for games of chance at country fairs; today they are valued as collector's items.

A clear fire for boiling, a strong fire for roasting" was the old rule; and with wood-fed stoves used to cook three and often four meals a day, old-time kitchens became insufferably hot. To keep the heat from circulating to other rooms of the house during warmer months, "back" or "summer" kitchens were eventually added to the homes, and as stoves became less expensive, an extra one was placed in the back kitchen. Some families simply "moved out the stove" for the summer months (another backbreaking chore for the men), thus freeing the kitchen of its heat and dust. In winter, though, the wood stove - and earlier, the fireplace - made the pioneer kitchen the cosiest room in the house.

The kitchen was the real "live in" room of the pioneer house, as it still is in many rural homes, mainly because it was the most comfortable room. Perhaps, too, because the women had to work so constantly in the kitchen, everyone gathered there - often sitting around the big harvest table. The table was not simply a dining board; much preparation of meals, children's homework, and daily household chores - including the ironing - were accomplished on its scrubbed top.

In every early Canadian kitchen, a bench or couch of some kind could also be found. It might be a bench bed, a settle, a tramp bed, or a flop bench, but it was always a sturdy handmade structure, cumbersome to move. And usually, as was the case with most heavy furniture, after years of standing in the same place, it wore hollows in the old pine floor.

The bench was a convenient spot for the man of the house to grab a catnap before chores; it might also be pressed into use as a spare bed for an itinerant tradesman or a benighted traveller. If it were a settle, which opened out at night to reveal a mattress of straw and a box beneath for concealing bed covers during the day, it might serve as a bed for several children. Smaller children were often required to sleep crosswise on a large bed, but on frosty nights they seldom minded, for the more children, the cosier. If the settle were especially long, a few of them might sleep with their heads at the "head" of the bed and the others with their heads at the "foot" of the bed.

Unlike the kitchen, the austere parlour of the earlier home was usually closed off, and opened only on special occasions – a visit from the clergyman, a wedding or funeral, a Sunday-evening call from a beau. It was hardly conducive to amorous

advances, however. The beau often sat in miserable, thumb-twiddling silence while his shy belle played the harp or organ, and Ma, Granny, or Great Aunt Matilda rocked near by with her knitting.

"Look behind the parlour door" was frequently the answer to the question "Where did you put the new such and such?" All very special acquisitions were kept in "the room", as the parlour was often called. Some people can still recall the clothes mangle being stored in the parlour between washings, under a specially made cover; or perhaps it was the new churn or the ice cream freezer. In one particular family with five hungry boys, the doughnut crock was concealed there.

Even the good set of harness was, in many cases, stored in the parlour, or else hung up the back stairway, in the hall, or in a back bedroom, rather than in the mildew-producing stable. For, after all, the replacement of oxen by horses had meant a great outlay of precious cash, or a very special "trade", in order to obtain leather harness, and this harness was expected to last many years.

Pine was a favourite with many Canadian builders and furniture makers, because of its prevalance and its ease in handling and cutting. Many pioneers became so weary of looking at pine furniture, though, that they "comb-varnished" it (using a haircomb) or "feather-painted" it with a goose wing to resemble mahogany or other hardwood. In older homes, there are still tucked-away bedrooms with rug-covered pine floors that show, around the edges, an early coat of yellow-ochre powder paint.

So durable is pine that it has been known to lie immersed in water for a hundred years without ill effects; it is not so durable to wear, though. Pine rockers on an old family cradle are said to have required replacement for each new infant. Sometimes, to prevent wearing of the wood, leather coverings were fitted over the rockers, or they were fashioned of hardwood instead.

And at least one rocking chair, often of pine, was found in every early home. It not only rocked away the frustrations of a fussy child in the arms of mother or grandmother, but also lessened the tensions of the adult who did the rocking.

Many early Canadian homes had a downstairs bedroom, often known as the "borning room" because in it babies were usually brought into the world. It was also pressed into use as an infirmary in case of an accident or long illness, because of its convenience and proximity to the kitchen.

In most cases the "borning room" was the bedroom of the parents, who usually slept downstairs to keep an eye on the fire during cold winter months. Also, since this room benefitted from the heat of the nearby fire, a cradle was often kept here for the youngest child to sleep in.

Many of the old-time baby cradles were built with a "hood" to protect the infant's head from draughts in the cold house. Babies might sleep in these cradles up to the age of two years. If a new baby arrived before the older child was ready to "leave the nest", or in the event of twins, the cradle hood could be sawn off and a child laid at each end.

Another type of cradle was hung in a bed-level frame. This enabled a mother to reach out in the night to a whimpering child, without having to rise from a warm bed.

The "hand that rocked the cradle" was, in fact, often a foot; this is the reason that most rockers on the old cradles were built especially wide. Mothers could then continue sewing, knitting, or even churning butter while soothing a fretful baby.

Away up to your trundle bed," parents sometimes told their small children at bedtime. A trundle bed was a small bed that could be "trundled" or slid under a larger bed. It was most often found in guest rooms, for children visiting with their parents, or in hotels or halfway houses for a family sharing a room.

Bed warmers in an average household were not the long-handled, coal-filled brass beauties we may envision. In fact, those were relatively scarce in early Canada. Instead, most settlers heated rocks, bricks, or old irons and wrapped them in cloth or newspaper. Hot-water bottles made of crockery and heavy, water-filled ink bottles were also widely used.

Crockery "pigs", with corked snouts and flat bottoms, also filled with hot water, became popular, not just for use in beds but also in sleighs for winter travel. There was a special "foot-warmer" available for cold-weather travel as well - a box-like metal container with perforated lid, and a sliding drawer partly filled with live coals. With feet placed against its "holey" lid, and feet and body tucked under heavy travel rugs or a "buffalo robe", the traveller was ensured a certain degree of comfort. But again, the average person made his own foot-warmer from whatever was available - even from such dual-purpose objects as baked potatoes, corncobs, or oven-heated pieces of hardwood.

"Cleanliness is next to godliness," our ancestors believed, but it was often as difficult to achieve. Early homes could not boast of bathrooms as we know them. However, each bedroom was furnished with a wash basin, a jug for carrying water from the fire, lye soap, and a chamber pot, often referred to as a "thunder mug", kept under the bed or concealed in a lower section of the washstand for use during the night. Later bathroom sets included a toothbrush holder, a smaller jug, a cup, and a pail or "night chamber". The word "commode" often referred to a chair with a circular opening in the seat and space underneath for a night chamber; this was especially convenient for use in the sickroom.

Thoughtful housewives crocheted a ring to fit over the edge of the chamber lid, so that the lid could be replaced without that obvious and embarrassing noise. Known as a "silencer", it was particularly appreciated by overnight guests. The idea of guest towels has not changed much since early days. Pioneer women hung a fancy "show towel" over the family towel in the kitchen, and woe betide the family member who left tell-tale fingerprints on it!

For quick summer ablutions, a dish was placed on a bench on the verandah, stoop, or lean-to, or by the back kitchen door, with the rain barrel or a pail of water near at hand. The used water was splashed around the corner of the house - a practice that often caused an unsanitary slop, and encouraged flies. In winter, the water was sloshed into a pail, sometimes to be reused for a scrubbing job or else to be tossed far enough away that it would not create a dangerous "slide" upon freezing.

The outdoor toilet, more commonly called the "backhouse" or "privy", was usually partially concealed by lilacs or cedars, or in later years by a vine-covered trellis. Privies were built in three sizes: one-holer, two-holer, and three-holer. Many was the secret shared in the privacy of the privy, since a large family knew little other privacy. The mail-order catalogues and old

papers were destined for recycling in the backhouse, and articles read in old newspapers in the "library", as some families referred to it, were often discussed during the long evenings.

Woodpiles were part of the scenery in every yard in early days. Often the woodpile "happened" to be located between the privy and the house, perhaps so that the shy and modest could return with an armful of wood or an apronful of chips. The wood chips were as much as a foot deep around the edges of the woodpile. While softer woods like pine or cedar were used as kindling, the hardwood chips provided a quick fire for warming up a meal and, during the hot summer months, were preferable to a long-burning fire that would only add to the discomfort of an already hot and humid house.

Chopping wood was often a grandfather's chore, while the youngsters filled the ever-emptying wood-box. Just as rocking relieved the tensions of the women, wood-splitting served as an emotional outlet for the men-folk.

The Oxen Shed

"Black on the ridge, against that lonely flush,
A cart, and stoop-necked oxen; ranged beside,
Some barrels; and the day-worn harvest folk . . ."

- Charles G.D. Roberts

Oxen were a symbol of pioneer Canada. For would-be homesteaders arriving in Canada, one of the well-remembered first sights was a string of oxen pressed into service along the shore to haul the immigrant ship through the strong current as it neared Montreal.

Little could be accomplished in the bush without the aid of the patient and powerful oxen. Logs were moved to the cabin site by a yoke of oxen hitched to a heavy logging chain. As remaining trunks and branches were burned, the ashes were shovelled onto oxen sleds, to be hauled to the ash leach and dripped for lye to make potash or "black salts", which the settlers sold to dealers as a cash crop. When the land was sufficiently cleared of trees, the oxen were hitched to a "breaker plough" or "bull plough" to break up the rough virgin soil. The land was then "dragged" with a log pulled by oxen or horses in an attempt to level it somewhat before planting.

Before autumn turned to winter, a dedicated stockman "raised" a stable for the protection of his working oxen, with a loft above to house the meagre first harvests. Often, too, during summer months, an itinerant tradesman or temporary helper was "lofted" for the night in the oxen shed.

The later addition of a goose house was almost a status symbol, since the acquisition of a pair of geese raised the standard of living considerably. Eventually, too, pigs were kept over the winter, which meant the building of another shelter, aside from the usual straw stack. And finally a large grain barn was raised by communal effort.

Good fences make good neighbours" was a very old rural expression, and one not spoken lightly, because poor fences meant stray stock, which could and often did cause much strife between otherwise "good" neighbours. The picket fence usually pictured around century-old homes was not built solely to mark property lines, nor was it constructed as a thing of beauty. In the days when almost everybody, even in the rural villages, kept a horse, a cow, and perhaps a sheep, goat or pig, and small animals were allowed to roam, a durable fence with restraining pickets was an absolute must around the house and gardens.

Sturdy, less decorative fences were built around the planted areas in farming regions, to prevent stock from ruining all-important crops. There was quite a knack to erecting a fence that was stock-proof and storm-proof. In rural areas, in fact, you may still hear old-timers speak of fences that are "horse-high and hog-tight".

Cedar was mainly used in the construction of rail fences, and the fence might be split rail, straight rail, or snake (zigzag), which twisted sharply around trees and rocks. On a rocky farm, fences were often stone walls, built with stones cleared from the fields, with shrubs left as an extra deterrent against both domesticated and wild beasts. Stump fences were another product of land clearing. Pines that had once grown to heights we can now only imagine left huge, jagged stumps which were laboriously twisted out with the aid of oxen, often during "stumping bees"; piled with roots skyward, these stumps made almost impenetrable fences.

Nevertheless, the problem of "breachy" cattle (cattle that habitually broke through fences) became so great that "fence viewers" were hired in farming communities. Two men would travel from farm to farm to check the fences and determine if they were satisfactory, informing the careless farmer if his fences required mending.

"Dig through an ant hill and you will strike water," some old-timers claimed, believing that a large ant hill was always located on earth that covered water. Often, pump makers conveniently professed to be "water-witchers" or "diviners" as well; that is, they supposedly were endowed with the power to locate water underground by "stepping out" with a willow switch or wand in hand. If the switch twisted toward the ground and pulled the diviner's arm uncontrollably downward, then water flowed beneath. Some believed the plum branch to be most effective for divining (also called "dowsing") the whereabouts of water; others insisted that the stick must be a forked one.

Once the well site was established, the back-breaking task of digging to reach water level was begun. A pail was lowered into the well as the hole became deeper, and one man filled it with earth and allowed it to be pulled up and emptied by a helper above. A time-consuming and cramping chore - and grimly disappointing if water was not reached by a depth of fifteen or twenty feet. As a final step, the interior of the well was lined with rock and a rough covering was built over the excavation.

An open well often served the homesteader for many years. A rope, if available, or a hooked ash or ironwood sapling was secured to a long, perpendicular pole which rested on a sturdy forked post. This was known as a "sweep well" or a "well sweep". A bucket attached to the sapling or rope was "swept" into the well by simple manipulation of the long pole; it was of utmost importance that the "sweep" be well balanced. Also, if a sapling were used, an extra foot from the hook had to extend into the pail to prevent its floating off the hook. This also helped to force the bucket through the water for filling.

An equally popular method of hauling water from the open well involved the use of a "windlass" - a frame with a chain wound around the cross-bar and a crank to lower a bucket through a rough box of wood or stone into the well below.

Wooden pumps soon became available, and pump makers did a thriving business. Spruce or pine logs were hollowed out by means of a series of graduating-sized augers, and wooden spouts and handles were added. In later years these accessories were fashioned of iron. Although an advantage over the swing-and-dip or wind-and-pull methods, the wooden pump had one great disadvantage: the cylinder required defrosting on the coldest winter mornings, while thirsty stock voiced their disapproval.

With the advent of the picturesque water-pumping windmills on the Canadian landscape, the problem of watering stock in the "back forty" acres was considerably lessened. A large trough was set near by with another narrow, open-end trough carrying water from the pump to ensure its being filled with fresh water for stock at all times.

Horses or oxen? That was a question most farmers eventually asked themselves. At first the docile oxen were nearly indispensible, and they were preferable for bush work; they did not sink into mud or snow as readily as the smaller-hoofed horses, and when they did, they simply "flopped" until their owner could ease them out of their predicament. Horses, by contrast, immediately panicked and threshed about, which heightened the problem and frequently caused injury, not only to themselves but also to their would-be benefactor.

There was also the matter of harness. Whereas a pair of oxen required little more than a homemade yoke, a team of horses required expensive harness. And while horses proved speedier on better roads and much "lighter on their feet", most older stock-men claimed that oxen were stronger. Certainly they were steadier "on the pull".

The deciding factor was occasionally a sentimental one, although a pioneer farmer would never admit to this. Sometimes a farmer simply preferred his oxen, and considered them more sensitive animals. It was often said that, if one ox died, the other would refuse to work alone or with a different mate. And if there was strife between two oxen working together, flowers of the Yellow Loosestrife placed on their wooden yoke was believed to calm them.

Eventually horses won out, however. Soon they were discussed just as automobiles are today and, in work horses, a "spanking team" of fast walkers was always admired. As a good horseman will tell you, a young team allowed to trot habitually during their training period would never become a brisk-walking team. This could be quite important when a heavy load of logs or ice had to be moved some distance during the cold winter days.

And a good horseman seldom carried a whip. The old expression "keep your whip in the oat box" meant to replace the whip with an extra feed of oats, sure to speed up a horse or team.

As soon as a settler's finances or bargaining power permitted, a cow - often with a calf "at foot" - was purchased and a herd was gradually built up. Milk, with cream for butter, was an important farm commodity. For a cow to "go down in her milk" or "go dry" for no obvious reason was nothing short of a calamity, and in summer this was often blamed on the gentle milk snake.

Although there has been much controversy over whether milk snakes actually remove milk from a cow, there are still rural people who claim to have seen this occur. One believer described how, on several occasions, he watched a small milk snake balance itself on a few inches of its tail to extract the milk. The cow not only submitted to this but, uncomfortably full by late afternoon, would return to the same pasture corner each day to be relieved of the excess milk in her udder.

The old saying "Root, hog, or die!" was more than an expression; it was a fact. In the days of early settlers, pigs were expected to forage for themselves during summer and fall, and usually became fat on nuts and roots in the woods. Often they became quite wild, frightened the children, and would devour unwary chickens. Old records tell us, in fact, that some pioneers used the then-common passenger pigeons to fatten up their pigs.

In many areas, pork was the main source of meat, for early settlers could not afford to use their useful oxen or valuable wool-producing sheep for food. Also, because of wild predators, game was not as plentiful as is generally supposed.

Geese were the most practical fowl for early settlers; they required little care and could forage for themselves from spring until freeze-up. Their size meant a substantial meal. The feathers were valuable for dusting and for filling pillows and ticks, and the quills for administering medicine and for making quill pens. (Only six feathers from a goose were said to be suitable for these pens, and the early teachers and office workers were expected to fashion their own, using a small jack-knife or pen knife, as it came to be called.) Also, goose fat was mixed with turpentine, rubbed on the chest, and covered with warm flannel, as a common remedy for colds.

"Plucking bees" meant a neighbourly get-together in great-grandmother's day on the farm. A goose did not need to be killed in order to be plucked. Instead, a sack was placed over its head to avoid painful pecks and a portion of the down was removed for pillows and feather ticks. Apart from the indignity suffered, this was not a painful operation; most waterfowl pluck the down from their breasts as a nest lining.

Guinea fowl helped provide the family with eggs and meat. They were sometimes kept as guardians of earlier barnyards, rather than dogs, for they set up a great commotion whenever strange people or animals appeared. Some have even been known to take to the air in pursuit of a chicken hawk, and one particular guinea is said to have fought to its death with a fox in an effort to protect the barnyard flock.

Gardeners considered the guineas to be less destructive than other breeds of fowl because, although their appetite for bugs was voracious, they were not attracted to the vegetables and fruit as were other poultry. They did like buckwheat, though, and their constant cry, resembling the word "buckwheat", could become quite monotonous.

The plaintive call to "whip poor Will", wafting from the woods at dusk, was a familiar sound to the early bush settlers. So plentiful were these birds that they would often call from their nocturnal perch on a windowsill. Many people believed that, to ensure that corn would reach maturity by harvest time, it must be planted before the whippoorwills stopped calling in late spring or early summer.

Fields of wheat were laboriously planted by hand, as the farmer trudged across stump- or rock-dotted land carrying a bag of grain over one shoulder, and "broadcasting" the grain - tossing it by handfuls on the loosened earth, in the hope that it would take root and mature to provide bread for the family table.

One popular type of wheat grown was buckwheat, an early crop we seldom hear of today. It was ground into a rich white flour used in buckwheat cakes, mush, and other dishes. The children liked to nibble on it during long walks or to "pop" it in a heavy iron pan over the fire on winter evenings. It also provided feed for poultry and offered bees a sweet nectar for buckwheat honey. The straw was poor, though, and the grain was usually considered to be too rich for stock feed.

Harvesting, in early years, meant cutting the grain with a grain cradle or scythe. Usually the women followed along behind the men to bind the sheaves, and often it was the chore of young children to "ready the bands". A few deft twists with these straw strands would tie a sheaf securely until it was time to draw the harvest to a stack or shelter.

The tripod method of stacking and drying was used a great deal in early Canada. Hay was often stacked within the confines of a three-legged construction and pulled to the top of the "mow" with the aid of a horse. In much the same manner, in later years, it was hauled to the top of a well-built stack or up into a haymow inside the barn.

The Indians had taught settlers to stack and season wood in the tripod, or tepee, style, so that air and sunshine could keep the wood comparatively dry before buildings were available to protect it. In much the same way, stooks of grain were formed;

three sheaves were placed strategically so that air could circulate through them but wind could not easily dislodge them. In the event of a rain storm, the stooks must be again "turned out", that is, separated and laid out to dry, then re-stooked to await threshing or else thrown onto the wagon directly from the ground.

Most women, even in the backwoods clearings, longed for "hyacinths to feed thy soul". Lonely for old haunts and familiar flowers, they sent home to Europe for herb and flower seeds. Then, each succeeding year, they carefully saved the dried seeds and, where possible, divided roots to propagate the species. Eventually they were able to domesticate many types of wild shrubs that bore edible fruits, but in the meantime they gathered the plentiful wild fruits which they dried, preserved, or transformed into wine.

Early horticulturists found that a plant slip would take root more readily if they placed a few grains of wheat into the earth with it. Later, when they began to transplant fruit trees about their homes, they also tossed a peck of grain into the hole with the tree. This kept the earth loose for the slower-growing tree.

The settlers also soon learned to graft tree limbs successfully, which proved more effective and "true" for fruit than propagating by seed. At first they used a mixture of cow manure, clay, and hair as a healing compound to cover the exposed joints, then later developed a formula containing four parts rosin, two parts beeswax, and one part tallow (although some people preferred linseed oil to tallow). They would dip a cloth into this mixture as it cooled and then tie the cloth firmly over the joined sections of the boughs.

According to an old belief, a farmer who cut down a hawthorn tree would be sure to lose stock within the year. Since farm animals were precious, this notion saved many a bush from destruction. Similarly, the rowan tree, or mountain ash, was believed (especially by Irish settlers) to keep away the "banshees" - long-haired, wailing female spirits said to appear as forerunners of death. Many settlers also planted a Farewell Tree (Sweet Viburnum or "Sheep Berry") at the gate, because it supposedly brought good luck and Godspeed to a member of the household off on a journey.

The Rain Barrel

"To talk of the weather, it's nothing but folly,
For when it rains on the hill, it shines in the valley."

- Sir John Benham

So went the old proverb; yet in the days when most work was accomplished out-of-doors, and the weather determined a day's activities, everybody did talk of the weather. People in those days were generally more aware of life around them. They observed close connections between the vagaries of the weather and the actions of animals, insects, and birds. They watched carefully for "natural weather signs" - a change in the colour of the sky, for instance, or even a sudden attack of rheumatism. And often, in an attempt to remember all they had learned about the weather, they transformed the information into predictions, rhymes, and chants.

Rain, perhaps, was the element most closely observed. On pioneer farms, long before the age of complex irrigation systems, a rainfall meant a watering of the crops. To farmers' wives it meant a full rain barrel - and clean, fresh rainwater for laundry, cleaning, and in some homes even for cooking. Young and old alike would sit and soak their feet out by the rain barrel in summer months; besides being very relaxing, regular footbaths were essential when people worked in the fields or walked over dusty trails.

It is not surprising, then, that most of the old-time weather predictions concerned rain. The rain barrel would be filled by

morning, it was claimed, if the cat slept with its nose in the air, or preened behind its ears; if the dogs were seen eating grass; or if the pigs frolicked more than usual about the straw stack or carried twigs and straw in their mouths for a dry bed. Wild rabbits, usually nocturnal nibblers, seen feeding in the afternoon, fish biting exceptionally well, and cattle going "loco" in the evening were further signs of an approaching storm.

An extra trough would be set out beside the rain barrel to catch an overflow if the new moon held the old moon in its arms; if the horns of the moon turned downward; if distant objects appeared closer (damp air being more transparent than dry air); or if the outside of the barrel or a wooden bucket were sweating.

Birds and barnyard fowl inspired other rainy-weather predictions. According to one old chant, "If a rooster crows before going to bed, he'll get up in the morning with a wet head." Turkeys, which normally preferred to sleep outside on a high perch or in a tree, would head for indoor roosts if a storm were approaching. And if hens rushed for shelter at the beginning of a rainfall, only a shower was predicted, but if they continued to peck out-of-doors, you could expect an all-day rain.

Robins, always lovers of rain, were said to sing their cheeriest notes before or during a downpour. Cardinals whistling in spring would bring rain within a day, and especially noisy bluejays also meant wet weather. Swallows flying low, crows soaring high, and birds congregating on fences or branches before migrating season were all certain signs of rain.

Long walks and slow drives provided time for a leisurely study of the skies, and alert travellers came up with more wet-weather predictions: A sun shower always brings a rainbow, but it also brings more rain at the same hour on the following day. Rain inevitably follows a yellowish sunset. If the sun sets behind strangely coloured clouds, slashing rain is certain. And water drawn up by the sun through streaky clouds seldom fails to descend as raindrops.

For the more poetic, there were numerous couplets regarding the weather: "When the dew is on the grass, rain will never come to pass." "When the wind is in the east, 'tis good for neither man nor beast." "The wind from the south has rain in its mouth." "Rain will pour if Owl hoots from the hollow; if he hoots from the hill, dry weather will follow." "Mackeral sky, now wet, now dry." "Rain before seven, sun before eleven." "Ring around the moon brings a storm soon." And, finally, perhaps the oldest and most quoted: "Red sky at night, shepherd's delight; red sky in the morning, sailor take warning."

Looks like an open fall," hopeful homesteaders would tell one another, or, "Good in September, goes on to December!" An open fall - that is, long-lasting autumnal weather with little or no snow - meant ample time after harvest to make further preparations for the winter months ahead.

Winter stood for "wood, water, and weariness" to the old-timers, who were above all "hewers of wood and drawers of water". Chopping a jagged hole in a frozen creek or pond to lug water to the house and stable, or herding shivering stock over a snowy path to the watering hole, was cold, time-consuming work. Defrosting a wooden pump often necessitated lifting out the entire pump with attached rod before the ice could be carefully chipped away.

According to an old saying, the first snowfall was simply a warning that the real immobility of winter was only a month away; an early snowfall meant an early winter.

A snow that seemed to fall from all directions meant more to follow; snow clinging to the trunks of trees would soon be covered by more snow. Sudden gusts and roars in the fire were another sign of snow, and flocks of snowbirds always preceded a storm.

Old-timers often spoke of a "robin snow" - a snow following the return of the spring birds - and of a late "sugar snow", which meant a further run of sap to maple-sugar harvesters.

Summer droughts resulted in poor harvests and often near famine in new settlements. In the bush country, wind did little harm, except in case of a forest fire, but on Canadian prairies wind played havoc with crops and even removed topsoil from the fields.

A cool breeze, followed by a hot breeze, would cause an observant weather-wizard to comment, "We're sure in for a dry spell!"

The Harvest Table

"Beside her oven of clay and stone she stands
Where smouldering logs of pine and spruce are glowing . . ."

– Frank Oliver Call

The "daily bread" was simple yet sufficient in early homes. The harvest table, with a long bench on either side and a chair at each end, was usually well-laden for the large families of yesterday. But, come the harvesting or a raising bee, a real "groaning board" appeared almost overnight. Special dishes were prepared from fruits and vegetables that had been "saved for harvest-time".

In a household which did not include grown daughters or an aunt or grandmother, neighbour women usually came to assist with the cooking for perhaps a score of men, or, in the event of a "raising bee", sometimes up to one hundred! As more farmland was cleared and harvests became more abundant, it was practical to exchange help for harvesting the grain and, later in the season, the corn.

If the family was large, two sittings were necessary, with the family members, of course, comprising the second sitting. Families were accustomed to this, for nobody was of more importance than the neighbours (unless it was the clergyman, who was always served first).

"Don't go away hungry, eat up and give the place a good name!" guests were urged by their host. The old people, when invited to partake of a casual meal, felt it was polite to decline, but still expected to be coaxed.

25

They might insist they were unable to stay for supper, and even while pulling a chair up to the table, they would be remonstrating that they simply "could *not*" . . .

Earlier cooks could hardly depend on having fresh fruits, vegetables, and meat during the winter months. Advance preparation to preserve food was vital. Wild berries, for instance, were gleaned and then dried or "put down" in jars.

Refrigeration took many forms. As often as possible, the carcasses of larger animals, used for meat, were processed in late fall after freeze-up, when a thaw no longer seemed likely. Entire carcasses were often hung outside in a spot where they would be safe from predators, and were cut up and used as required. In the event of a sudden thaw, the meat was taken down and cut into family-meal sizes, then packed in a barrel or box with wet snow, which would quickly freeze around it.

Sometimes a small stream flowing near the house was channeled through a ditch dug into the earthen cellar floor, so buckets of perishable food could be conveniently lowered into the cold water. Wells and springs provided a similar means of refrigeration.

In later years, river ice was cut into blocks and hauled to an "ice house", where it was packed carefully with sawdust or cut straw. Individual blocks could then be extracted with large ice tongs when needed during the warm summer months.

Since ice harvesting was a very cold, laborious task, the ice was kept primarily for preserving fresh foods. It was a very special occasion indeed when the precious block was broken off and crushed in a heavy bag in preparation for the making of home-made ice cream.

Ice cream has been made in many different ways. One unusual recipe, handwritten in the margin of an old Canadian cookbook, was simply entitled "winter ice cream". It called for one and one-half cups of cream, well beaten, one-half cup of sugar, two eggs, and flavouring. The method? "Hang on the clothesline and freeze."

By the mid nineteenth century, a woman had invented the first hand-turned ice cream freezer, and recipes became more complicated.

Custard Ice Cream

Beat two eggs. Add three cups of cream, one cup of milk, one heaping cup of sugar, and one tablespoon of vanilla. Mix thoroughly and chill. Pour the chilled custard into the freezer can, set it in the freezer pail, and pack ice around it, sprinkling the ice with coarse salt while packing. Cover, fasten the freezer can, and turn the crank slowly until it becomes difficult. Then open the can and remove the dasher. Scrape the cream from the sides, mix until smooth, close the can, and drain off melted ice from the outer bucket. Add fresh salt and ice, covering the can. Wrap a cold blanket around the freezer and let it stand for two hours, then serve. In very hot weather, the salt and ice may need to be renewed three times; keep the blanket cold and wet with brine from the freezer.

Food that was not frozen for future use had to be preserved by other means. Fish was often hung and thoroughly dried, but frequently it was cooked, shaken from the bones, and placed between layers of salt and pepper and cooked, mashed potatoes, in barrels or boxes for freezing. Pork might be fried and packed into a crock, with the rendered fat poured over each layer to seal out the air, then stored in a cool place. Frequently, too, meat was preserved in brine. A large quantity could be prepared at one time, as this old recipe indicates.

Brine for 100 Pounds of Pork or Beef

Eight pounds of salt
Two ounces of salt petre
Two pounds of brown sugar
One ounce of black pepper
Four gallons of water
One ounce of soda

Remove the meat from the bones, rub pieces with salt and let stand overnight. Then wipe off excess salt and pack in a barrel. Prepare the brine, boil for a few minutes, adding the soda just before removing from the heat. Skim and pour the brine, still hot, over beef, but allow to cool for pork.

The pork barrel was set on a platform at the foot of the basement steps. Each morning a woman of the household reached into the tingling brine to select a piece of salt pork for dinner or supper. To remove excess saltiness, the meat was "steeped" or par-boiled (that is, simmered in a mixture of milk and water for an hour or so), drained and simmered in a fresh mixture. According to the old cooks, salt meat should never be boiled; they believed that "simmering draws out the salt but boiling drives it in". The meat was then usually fried; but hams were often simmered for hours, and often smoked by hanging inside a chimney or in a smoke-house for several days.

Even eggs had to be preserved, for hens sheltered in cold buildings seldom laid during the winter months. That first spring egg, probably found frozen, was always triumphantly carried in and thawed in cold water for use in baking.

In order to have eggs on hand for winter baking, they had to be "put down" when plentiful. Dozens were packed in layers in a wooden box, along with oats or bran to exclude the air; some people greased them with mutton tallow first, as an added precaution. Another method of preserving eggs for a short time was to place them in a crock of salt, the small ends pointing downward.

According to Great Aunt Sally, "Beware the egg that doesn't sink in a pan of cold water," and "An egg is as good as a pound of meat." She also declared that if you threw egg shells into the fire before the baking came out of the oven, it would not turn out well. Some old-time cooks insisted that a wooden spoon should be used for scrambling eggs; others said nothing works as well as a three-pronged fork.

Although pumpkins were considered a staple food, the left-overs were never fed to the hens. The old people believed, and perhaps rightly so, that pumpkins would "take the hens off their lay". To discourage a hen from "setting", if it was hoped she would continue to lay eggs instead, she was sometimes placed in a bag and hung on the clothes line for a few hours, or stood in a pan of water within a box. And according to Great Aunt Sally, "If you 'set' a hen on a Sunday, she will hatch nothing but roosters!"

Bread, the "staff of life," almost without

exception was baked in the individual home. It did not necessarily follow, though, that each homemaker turned out "crackling good bread", no more than every woman forced to fashion the family's supply of clothing was a "born" seamstress.

Most of the settlers grew their own hops for making yeast (and in some areas, beer). A "barm" was often made by boiling a handful or two of hops until juice was extracted, then straining and adding salt before setting aside to cool. Enough flour to make a thin batter was beaten in and this "barm" was put aside to rise, with extra flour added on baking day.

The bread dough was "set" at night - that is, mixed and kneaded until elastic, then placed in a floured bowl or "dough box" (near a fire during the winter months) to rise to double its bulk overnight. In the morning it was punched down, kneaded for another fifteen minutes or so, formed into loaves, and allowed to rise in the pans before baking.

Butter churns were constructed in many different shapes and sizes. Perhaps the most fascinating one was the dog-powered butter churn; a dog "ran" within a large wheel, causing a pulley to turn the paddle inside an attached churn. Stories are told of dogs which would disappear at the first sign of churning preparations; another might thoroughly enjoy it, perhaps urged on by a young master impatient to get off to the old swimmin' hole with his pooch.

In an emergency, enough butter for a meal could be churned in a quart jar by simply shaking one-half quart (or more) of cream back and forth by hand, occasionally opening the lid to permit gas to escape.

"Come, butter, come! Come, butter, come! Peter's standing by the gate, waiting for a butter cake. Come, butter, come!" So went the old churning chant. People said that when the "plop" of the cream became "pa-lop", butter globules were forming, but churning should continue for a few minutes more. Then the buttermilk would be drained off, the butter rinsed with cold water, and *all* the buttermilk pressed out with a paddle or spatula. The butter would be rinsed again until perfectly clear, drained well, and a pinch of food colouring added (juice from grated carrots or dandelion blooms worked fine).

Baking powder, a combination of bicarbonate of soda and citric acid, was invented before 1850 by an English chemist, Alfred

Bird, but was not commercially available in Canada until after Confederation. A simple homemade variety was often used instead. The recipe consisted of thirty ounces of powdered cream of tartar, fifteen ounces of bicarbonate of soda, and five ounces of flour, mixed well and kept thoroughly dry. Three teaspoons was recommended for use with each quart of flour.

A doughnut crock was found on almost every pantry shelf, and there was usually a mother or grandmother who kept it well filled.

The secret in making grease-free doughnuts, according to an old family recipe, was to use cream instead of milk as the liquid. The cream was said to prevent the dough from absorbing too much fat while frying. Some old cookbooks advocated adding a pinch of ginger for the same reason.

Another secret was to keep the temperature of the fat uniform. If it was too cool, the doughnuts would absorb more fat; if it was too hot, they might brown before they had risen properly. To test the fat for "readiness", a small portion of the dough was dropped into the fat; if it rose quickly to the top, the temperature was right.

The last of the batch consisted of the

"holes", or else of "twisters", made by entwining the ends of a single strand of dough in opposite directions until the twists met in the centre of the strand and twisted back to form a double twist. There was quite a knack to entwining correctly; a properly twisted twister would not unwind during frying.

Risen Doughnuts

Take one pint of simmering cream, two cups of sugar, one-half cup of butter, one-half pint of yeast or an envelope of yeast granules dissolved in one cup of warm water, and two eggs. Beat together the eggs, butter, and sugar, then pour in the cream. Add flour until thick enough to roll but still soft. Let it rise twice, cut out the doughnuts, and let rise again. Brown in deep, smoking-hot lard and drain on absorbent paper. When cool, store in a crock and hide on a pantry shelf or behind the parlour door.

White sugar was scarce and expensive; brown sugar, molasses, maple sugar or syrup, and honey - often wild - were used extensively.

Molasses was imported. Sometimes it was poured into the hold of a ship and used as ballast, later to be sold in barrels. Often, too, dishes travelled safely to Canada sunk in containers of molasses. Sometimes called treacle, the old-time molasses was simply a syrup drained off during the making of sugar.

Honey from the hives of wild bees was said to be very strong-tasting. The first honey of the season came from the blossoms of the basswood tree and was especially sought after, and buckwheat blossoms provided the bees with a later crop (although the dark, rich buckwheat honey was not in great demand in earlier days). Comb honey (that is, honey left in the wax forms or "combs") was always a gourmet's delight, but sometimes it was extracted. A great pan of honey comb might be set in a lowering oven, or a clean bag of honey comb could be hung in a warm place, until the honey drained into a wide-mouth jar or pail set beneath. Eventually, metal honey extractors took the messiness out of this chore.

Maple sugar making, learned from the Indians, soon became an important Canadian activity. In early years more sugar was used than syrup. Sap gatherers learned, through years of experience, that a good yield of sap almost always meant a poor year for hay. Another observation was that, after the first frog chorus, the sap pails could be taken down; the season was finished.

A "sugaring off" was a social occasion, enjoyed by adults and children alike. The sap was boiled down to a thick syrup and poured in strips onto clean snow to harden, then pulled like taffy.

Start the day with a good breakfast" was an unwritten rule in early families. A good stiff "plate of porridge" was started at night before the fire was "let out". The pot was left on the back of the wood stove or shoved well to the side on the trammel over the fireplace, ready to be reheated when the fire was stirred up very early the next morning.

At least one old spoon in every household was worn down to half its original size as a result of daily use as a scraper of porridge pots! Once clean, the porridge pot very often became the potato pot, and so on.

Grandma Armstrong's Irish Potato Cakes

Boil a good-sized pot of potatoes over the breakfast or noon fire, drain, and thoroughly "pound" them. Add a dash of milk and knead in flour until quite stiff. Add chopped onion, a bit of butter, and form into a loaf, then coat with flour and chill. At supper time, slice the loaf thickly and brown the slices in a well-greased, heavy iron pan (pork fat is best). Serve with meat and vegetables.

Sauerkraut was made by filling a barrel with layers of cabbages and layers of salt. Then, judging from the old folk songs and tales handed down, the cabbages were often tramped with the feet, in the same way that grapes were prepared for wine making.

In some parts of the country, bread dough was also "kneaded" thoroughly with the aid of clean, bare feet. In later years, "kneaders" became popular; they were made in the form of tin pails, with a bent, steel arm that turned the dough until it formed a ball around the "hand". Directions on the fitted lid explained method of use.

Horseradish added zest to many pioneer meals, and once established in a corner of the yard or garden, no amount of discouraging would remove it. Often it was packed in a box of sand for use during the winter months.

A teaspoonful of horseradish grated into a pan of milk would keep the milk sweet for several days. Horseradish bruised and bound over the jaw and left overnight was said to ease a toothache.

Pickled Horseradish

Put two and one-half cups of grated horseradish in a bowl with two table spoons of sugar, about a teaspoon of salt, and two cups of cold vinegar. Mix well and pour into clean jars or crocks. It may be used at once but is better if left for a week or two.

Rhubarb, or "pieplant", became an early culinary standby in the Canadian garden. Old-time rhubarb was large-leaved and coarse; apple-green with tinges of red, it was often called Giant or Apple Rhubarb. It could be eaten "out of hand", sometimes with a little sugar since it was quite sour, but usually it was made into a favourite thirst-quenching drink or a delicious pie.

Rhubarb was considered by many to be a "kill or cure", because a remedy for indigestion was concocted from rhubarb and soda. The roots were sometimes infused as a dye to lighten the colour of hair. Even the leaves had their uses, although they contained a deadly poison. Dried, crushed, and then boiled, the leaves were used as an insecticide by early Scottish settlers. And many generations of children tried, although unsuccessfully, to "fly" using rhubarb leaves as wings.

Mamma's Rhubarb Juice

Boil two cups of cut rhubarb in three quarts of water for half an hour. Strain through a jelly bag and put in one cup of sugar. Bring to a rolling boil, cool, add lemon juice if handy, and bottle. Makes two cups of juice.

Filling for Rhubarb Pie

Mix one cup of chopped rhubarb, the yolks of two eggs, one and one-half cups of sugar, and two tablespoons of flour. Pour the filling into an unbaked pie crust.

Mamma Andrews' Pumpkin Pie

3 cups stewed pumpkin
4 eggs, beaten lightly
2 cups white sugar
2 teaspoons each of cinnamon and ginger
1 teaspoon of salt
3 cups of milk
6 tablespoons of cornstarch

Force the fresh, cooked pumpkin through a sieve into a cooking pot. Add the beaten eggs, sugar, salt and spices. Mix the cornstarch and milk together and add to pumpkin mixture. Cook over low heat until thick and pour into unbaked pie shells. Add latticed pie crust if desired and bake in a very hot oven. "The secret is in the second cooking," Mamma always said.

In days gone by, when meals were planned according to provisions on hand, pies were often a combination of several wild fruits. In a good apple season, apples were added to almost every desert dish.

Pioneer pumpkin pies were frequently made in much the same way as apple pies, with the pumpkin grated or cut thinly and layered with sugar and spices, because the milk required for the custard version was scarce in fall and winter. In a season when carrots were plentiful and pumpkins were not, carrots might be substituted. They are sweeter than pumpkin, so a carrot pie required less sugar.

Berry picking was a serious business when each year wild berries were transformed into shelves full of winter goodness. In most areas, the wild strawberries were the earliest and the very "essence of summer". "Doubtless God could make a better berry but doubtless God never did!" was a popular quote. Strawberries were followed by the later berries, and the raspberry harvest usually overlapped into the blueberry season.

The smaller, sweet, ground blueberries hid shyly under leaves, rocks, and often poison ivy; a pailful was well earned and thoroughly enjoyed, even during a noon-hour break on picking days. Berries were added to buttered and sugared bread for a delightful lunch dessert, with musical accompaniment from the buzzing tree toads. And there was the lunch pail, emptied, to be refilled with juicy blueberries.

The big, dark blueberries, though, grew on high bushes right smack in the middle of a bog. And the thought of fresh blueberry pie usually overcame any fear of snakes and crawling creatures (which were probably nonexistant anyway). The berry-gatherer simply pulled on well-greased Wellington boots and held the berry basket high.

Blueberry "pickers" - wooden, slatted scoops, later made of metal - were once available. These were quick and great for making a "clean sweep" of a bush, but unfortunately they also picked many of the big green berries, leaving none to ripen, which was of course impractical.

Elderberries were one of the more important wild fruits of the backwoods settlers and were used in the making of pies, wine, jam, and jelly. A few were often added to pancakes and muffins, and they were sometimes dried for winter use. Elderberries are very seedy, but a handful tossed into a pie shell and heaped with sliced apples gives a pie a lovely pink colour and distinctive flavour. An excellent soup could also be made from them.

A three- or four-pronged table fork or a clean comb made a most efficient tool for removing the berries from their stems. Children enjoyed a day of elderberry picking, too, and were sure to gather extra stems to fashion into "pea-shooters". They forced the pith, a dry, rubbery substance, into balls to load into the hollow stems as harmless ammunition.

Fruit trees soon became available from early nurseries and cherries in many forms became a favourite dessert. The old-fashioned cherry pitter worked well for these domesticated cherries but Great Granny found that her hair pin separated the pit from the cherry equally as well.

Wild choke cherries were plentiful and a real source of vitamins for youngsters of earlier days. Sometimes a child would claim a tree or a clump of trees for the season; the temporary choke-cherry-brown teeth at the close of the day were a sure sign of a good claim.

Come supper time, a pailful was brought home to be manufactured into wine.

Mamma Andrews' Choke Cherry Wine

Take any quantity of pitted cherries and cover with boiling water. Crush the fruit. Let stand for fifteen or twenty days, then strain carefully. Put one cup of sugar to every two cups of juice, stirring over heat until the sugar is dissolved. Bottle and seal.

Butternut hunting was once a great autumn adventure. With humans and squirrels competing for the harvest, a big sack full of butternuts was considered ample reward for hours spent tramping over rocks and through woods. The large, oval-shaped butternuts, sometimes known as white walnuts, were not only used in baking but often were pickled whole, or eaten as a hand-to-mouth snack. (The old flatirons made convenient and effective nutcrackers.) Also, the butternut hulls provided a brownish-yellow dye that was used to colour homespun woollen garments.

Great Aunt Sally's Pickled Butternuts

Gather the nuts in July when they can be pierced easily with a pin and they are at their "right readiness" for pickling. Soak in salt water for a week, then drain. Rub off roughness. Add a teacup of salt, a tablespoon of powdered cloves and mace, mixed, and one-half ounce of allspice and peppercorns to each gallon of vinegar. May be used in a fortnight.

At a time when much energy was expended from daylight to dusk, adults in a family felt the need of a bedtime snack around the kitchen table or by the fire. A bowl of bread and milk, an apple, nuts, or a piece of buttered bread was considered a satisfying treat. While the men "had a pipe", the women prepared for the morning's task and "redd up" the table.

Reddin' Up

"I could be busy all the day
Cleaning and sweeping the hearth and floor . . . "

- Padraic Colum

In the early Canadian homes, dishwashing followed every meal. Despite pictures of well-filled corner cabinets, most homes were frugally furnished, and a kitchen hutch held the few odd dishes the family owned. Only those essential for a meal were used – no separate bowls for salad or dessert. In fact, some of the old plates with deep bases were simply turned over after the first course so that dessert could be eaten from the clean underside. In most homes, egg cups were unthought of; a boiled egg was set down firmly on the breakfast plate, flattening the base for easy removal of the contents.

Eventually, most housewives acquired finer furnishings and a "good" set of china, which was treated with the care it deserved. For washing the china, a mixture was sometimes made from two and one-half pounds of washing soda, one pound of lime, one ounce of borax, and two ounces of pounded white resin dissolved in two and one-half gallons of heated rainwater. After this mixture cooled, it was allowed to settle and then was stored in jars for use as needed.

When the table was cleared and the dishes were "redd up", an "after cloth" was laid in the more genteel homes. Often this was an elaborate tablecloth, perhaps of handwoven fabric trimmed with tassles, or of linen decorated with drawn-work, or sometimes a fine crocheted cloth. A bowl of fruit or nuts or a vase of flowers might be centred on this cloth by the more artful housewife.

A copper kettle singing on the hearth, long considered a sign of good luck in England, became in Canada a sign of affluence as well. Copper utensils were also sought after for their convenience, because they were especially good conductors of heat. Proud of their copper pots, early housewives shone them until they gleamed, applying a paste of salt and vinegar with a dry piece of flannel and then rubbing vigorously.

House-proud pioneer women kept several goose wings about the house for dusting chores. One wing, with the end wrapped in flannel, always hung by the fireplace or wood-burning stove to swish away dust and ashes. Another was needed for the "good" furniture, such as a spinnet or dulcimer, and nothing swept down the stairs as effectively as the wing of a goose. In an emergency, one could even be used to fan embers into flames.

A clean goose wing was sometimes used for spreading butter atop loaves of freshly baked bread, and for dusting crumbs from the griddle (which was never washed in water). A wing was used for dusting flour from the baking board or table and for brushing out the oven.

When goose wings were not available, the feathers of other waterfowl were preferred to those of turkeys or hens for dusting chores, since the oil in these feathers held the dust rather than scattering it. Turkey feathers were also widely used as dusters, but would scorch more readily around the fire.

When the coal-oil lamp came into general use in the early 1860s, lamp chimneys were shone as energetically as the newly acquired copper kettle of earlier years. Each morning the lamp was filled with kerosene, and the chimney was cleaned with crumpled wet newspaper, old rags, or a feather duster, then carefully protected from dust with a cloth until evening. In later years, a paper bag was inverted over the lamp glass.

Lamp wicks were said to burn clear and bright if soaked in strong vinegar and dried thoroughly before use. Occasionally the burners, which held the chimney firmly in place, were simmered on the stove in a dish of strong soapsuds, or boiled in water strained from boiled beans or apple parings.

"Don't put the lantern on the table" was a common admonition after coal-oil lamps and lanterns came into use, and the chant "Lantern on the table, trouble in the stable" was also very well known. A lamp chimney was said to last much longer if it was first set in a pan of cold water and gradually allowed to come to a boil. It was also suggested that the lamp wick be turned well down before the lamp was blown out, to prevent the odour of oil and other disagreeable fumes. Sometimes, to add colour and interest, a small square of red flannel was added to the oil in the bowl of the lamp.

One of the most interesting types of lamps was the "sparking" lamp, which was small and squat and provided a minimum of light. When the lamp went out, so, presumably, did a suitor who was visiting. There was, in all probability, a chaperone near by to ensure that he did.

cleaning became a necessary tradition. The approach of winter had necessitated moving into the house such items as churns and wash tubs; the advent of spring meant their return to summer positions in the back kitchen, lean-to, or stoop.

The coming of spring also meant laundering bulky winter clothing, washing heavy curtains, beating thick rugs, airing quilts and feather mattresses, and scrubbing walls and ceilings smoked from winter fires. The hatches were unbattened, too. Windows and doors which had been closed for winter, with rags stuffed between the cracks, were pried open; and the "banking" of earth, built up about the base of the house at freeze-up to protect the root vegetables and keep out winter blasts, was removed.

Despite the hard work involved, pioneer women welcomed spring cleaning. It gave them a chance to shrug off winter doldrums, and to literally work out their frustrations. In short, spring housecleaning was an uproar, dreaded by men but thoroughly enjoyed by women.

As soon as early Canadians acquired sufficient belongings to clutter a house during the winter months, spring house-

Wood-burning stoves brought with them the meanest chore in choredom - the cleaning out of the stovepipes each month or so. When the stoves were used almost constantly, the pipes would soon become clogged with soot and ashes. This could, and often did, cause a dangerous chimney fire if the pipes were not regularly taken down and scraped out. The proximity of the pipes to the low ceilings was also very dangerous. It has been claimed that, in homes built after stoves became standard household equipment, ceilings rose ten feet to accomodate the stovepipes - an exaggeration, of course, but one containing a grain of truth.

According to old-timers, more people "sinned their souls" over pesky stovepipes than any other piece of household equipment. It took the "patience of Job and the wisdom of Solomon" to fit the stubborn pipes together again properly after they had been cleaned; a common table knife was eventually found to be very helpful for the task of fitting the pipes back together.

Making up the beds was no small task in a large rural family. Much shaking and turning of mattresses was necessary to guard against matting and to ensure a smooth "finish".

Mattresses and pillows of earlier days were filled with whatever material was available. Originally, and especially in the bush cabins, balsam boughs were spread on an elevated structure, with pillows "to match"; these were said to have been most pleasant and sleep-inducing. Later, "moose-munch" or beaver grass, shredded corn husks that had been dried in the sun, or even sawdust that had been carried from the mill or painstakingly saved from the woodpile were used. Straw was the most common; barley and rye straw were uncomfortable but were said to discourage mice, and wheat straw was considered less dusty than oat straw.

In order to prevent irritation from the straw, heavy ticking fabric was made into a mattress covering, or a heavy quilt was laid directly over the straw mattress, with sheets and blankets arranged over top. Soft beeswax, when available, was rubbed over the mattress ticking, in an effort to prevent straw from breaking through. By threshing time each year, the straw-filled ticks were pretty well reduced to chaff, and the old straw had to be replaced with newly threshed, fluffy, fragrant straw.

In the homes of families who kept barnyard fowl, mattress bags were often feather-filled. Indeed, feathers were even sometimes obtained from the passenger pigeons that flocked over pioneer grainfields by the hundreds. More ingenious homemakers created reversible ticks, presumably for the guest room. One side was filled with straw for the warm summer months while the reverse side was feather-filled for winter months; in between the layers was a heavy ticking material.

Each morning the feather ticks were flipped over three times and smoothed down with the aid of the broom. Some women used instead an especially designed smoother or "patter", not unlike the "peel" used for moving loaves of bread in and out of the oven.

The old-time rope bed springs tended to sag in the middle; one of the many chores of a pioneer child was to periodically "walk the springs". Around and around on the outer ropes he walked until the springs became taut again. The ropes could also be sponged or soaked to cause shrinkage; this was time-consuming, though, and involved extra work for the ever-busy adults. A type of winch was available for tightening these rope springs, but very few people were fortunate enough to own one.

The time of year and the height of water in the rain barrel usually determined when and how much laundry could be done in the early household. In winter, drying of heavy clothes and blankets was almost impossible,

so these were merely "aired" occasionally. Some wooden bedsteads were made with a "blanket roll" pole at the foot; the heavy quilts and blankets would be flipped over this and rolled back for a periodic airing. Finally, come spring, the bulky clothes and quilts could be thoroughly laundered or aired out-of-doors.

Fresh, "soft" water from the rain barrel was the best for working up suds for washing clothing (as well as for dishes and hair). On the old homesteads, it was also frequently the most available, usable water. No rain might mean no wash. Of course, if a river ran near by, the early washings could be done on its bank, with plenty of rinsing water at hand. Otherwise, washing water had to be lugged from the nearest site and heated over a fireplace, outdoor fire, or stove, while another tub filled in early morning was warming in the hot summer sun for rinsing purposes.

It was actually illegal, in the early days in Upper Canada, to hang on an outdoor clothesline a "mixed company" of men's and women's undergarments. Ladies' "unmentionables" were usually hung unobtrusively behind screens on indoor clothes racks.

According to early belief, not only was the sun a good bleaching agent, but so were the frost and the moonlight. An hour of morning sun was considered worth two hours of afternoon sun. Clothes to be bleached were spread on the grass or over a bush in summer, and on the clean snow in winter.

The old-time ironing board was simply a board with two or three old blankets wrapped around it and pinned securely in place. More often, the ironing board was merely an "ironing blanket" smoothed over the end of the old harvest table. An old cloth or newspaper was placed within reach for a trial run in case the iron was too hot (usually it was either too hot or too cold), and for wiping off any smoke streaks from the wood stove. A piece of beeswax, soap, or tallow wrapped between two pieces of flannelette was kept handy to rub the iron across occasionally for smoother movement.

The old hollow laundry irons were filled with red-hot coals or iron blocks. For smoothing lace, frills, and ribbons, a "gophering" or goffering iron was used; this was a short iron rod that was heated in the coals and then fitted into a clean iron sheath. "Crimping" irons, of two-part, corrugated construction for crimping or pleating an apron edge or a plain dust cap, were considered a luxury. Old ladies who

found one of these beyond their means would sit and crimp the edge of apron or cap with their fingers as they rocked and chatted. If the article had been carefully starched beforehand, this would make an effective decoration.

With the advent of the cook stove came the flatiron - an improvement, certainly, but since it was made entirely of iron, the handle became almost as hot as the base, and a holder had to be used with it. Flatirons had many uses apart from smoothing clothes. A heavy flatiron was often placed on the middle of a rug that was being braided, to help keep the centre flat, and two flatirons frequently took the place of an extra pair of arms when skeins of wool were being rolled into balls.

By the turn of the century, joy of joys, the "sad" iron appeared on the kitchen scene. Advertised as the cold-handle iron because its wooden handle could be detached while the iron was heating on the stove and then replaced for ironing, it was a decided improvement on the old flatiron.

The rain barrel was so valued as a "holder of water" for cooking, cleaning, and bathing that even in fall it was seldom moved from its settled-down spot at the corner of the house "under the drip". As winter approached, a large block of wood was shoved in the barrel so that the water would not freeze solid; after all, there was the January thaw to look forward to!

In summer, mosquito larvae, commonly called "wrigglers", often had to be strained off first, but usually a smart slap of the long-handled dipper on the surface of the water sent them squiggling to the bottom of the barrel.

When the heavy, awkward barrel was nearly empty, it was drained and cleaned. Unslacked lime and fresh water were added, and the barrel was rolled and rinsed thoroughly, or simply swished by hand and rolled.

Most settlers tried to save some water in the rain barrel for emergencies, such as a small fire. (Sometimes they prepared a mixture for extinguishing fires from twenty parts chloride of lime and five parts salt, to be dissolved in seventy-five parts water.) An empty rain barrel often necessitated drawing water from the nearest spring, or, later, the well. Human shoulder yokes with heavy buckets were specially made for the purpose, or else a pole with a whittled-out notch on each side, to prevent bucket handles from slipping, was fitted across the shoulders. Not only adults but children, too, were obliged to attend to this task.

Upon completion of the laborious laundry chore, water was destined for further cleansing. There was always a stoop, a back kitchen floor, or the privy to be scrubbed, perhaps using an old brick as a brush. The pioneer housewife used what was at hand; at a dry sink or on the kitchen windowsill near by, such pot scrapers as clam shells or pine cones might be found. Even though commercial pot scrapers soon became available in general stores throughout the country, the "Horsetail" plant, dried in the fall and tied into small bundles, was as widely used, and came to be called "scouring rush".

Diluted lye and pure sand, salt, or ashes were common cleansers for the pine floors, stoops, tables, and pots. Sand or wet sawdust was sprinkled on pine floors before sweeping to help keep down dust. Soap was seldom used on table tops because the housewives, who took great pride in their white "scrubbed top" pine tables, felt that it darkened them.

In pioneer days, the "broom that swept clean" - or otherwise - was often a splint broom, fashioned of a single piece of wood whittled down the handle into a broad base. Special "broom corn" was also grown. After drying, it was cut into broom-size lengths, bound together, and fastened with thongs of leather or cord to a stout stick. Horsehair brooms were used by a few housewives, but in a crude cabin an evergreen branch made a much more effective weapon against grime.

For many years, brooms were fashioned in the home, and broom-making became quite an art. Eventually, though, a broom-making machine came into use, and people began to buy from the broom-makers' shops that sprang up in almost every hamlet and village.

Woman's Work Was Never Done

"Pray tell me, can she spin?"

– James I

Pioneer housewives were said to have worn a path across the old pine floors as they spun their wool into yarn on the "walking" or "great" wheels. Three steps backwards, drawing out the yarn, and three steps forward, winding it onto the spindle. In the course of a day's spinning, they might walk as much as twenty miles! Often they set the spinning wheel out-of-doors in fine weather, not only to escape the heat of the house, but also to keep an eye on children and stock while they worked.

Most clothing, at least in remote areas, came from the flax spun by the women into linen threads and then woven into cloth, or from sheep's wool, spun into yarn to knit or weave into garments. Horsehair, mixed with sheep's wool in spinning, was said to make an almost unbreakable yarn. Wool from a dead sheep was useless for spinning purposes, as it immediately lost its elaticity. Left-over bits of broken wool were spun into a rough yarn known as "shoddy", for use in family homespuns only and never for "Sunday, go to meeting" clothes. Perhaps this explains why the word "shoddy" gradually came to describe a person of rough or less than upright character.

Similarly, the word "spinster" originally referred to any female spinner. But since this task often befell an unmarried sister or

aunt in the home, the word came to mean any unmarried woman. Most women were entirely dependent on relatives a generation or two ago, and felt a deep sense of family loyalty. Many remained spinsters because of a sense of duty toward an aged or invalid parent or toward a brother or father who required housekeeping services.

Besides the enormous task of spinning and weaving, housewives faced the never-ending chore of transforming fabric and yarn into clothing for their large families. Wardrobes in those days were not extensive; a "Sunday, go to meeting" outfit and some daily clothing was considered adequate, especially since this might be multiplied by ten or twelve family members. And of course, with so many children, clothing had to be "handed down" from one child to another. On the rare occasion when a child had a new garment made just for him, it was always designed at least one size too large, to ensure several years' wear. Housewives seldom discarded old knitted items such as shawls, for these could be unravelled to re-use the yarn, or saved to be made into rugs or afghans.

As cotton gradually found its way into Canada from the United States and became available through pedlars or in the local general store, many women began to purchase large quantities of it, finding it both time-saving and practical. The voluminous dresses they wore required seven or eight yards of material – which had taken a considerable amount of spinning and weaving before the age of "store-boughten" fabric.

In most homes, the dresses of the women and girls were fashioned from the same pattern and the same material; mother-and-daughter and big-and-little-sister outfits are not new by any means. To lengthen the life of their homespun dresses, women usually wore long, full aprons to "cover all" against the grime of household chores. These voluminous aprons also doubled as pot holders, and were handy to wipe a perspiring brow while standing for hours over a hot fireplace or wood stove. They were useful, too, for carrying chips for a quick fire, for holding eggs, baby chicks, goslings or ducklings, or garden produce, for a quick emergency dusting, or for swishing an errant hen from the garden or a pig from the orchard. Many's the tear-stained face wiped clean on a fold of granny's apron. And nothing would summon a man home for dinner more quickly than the silent signal of a wifely apron fluttering from a high perch or tied to the end of a good woman's broom handle.

A talent for "sewing a fine seam" was so necessary in the early home that a young lady would find it difficult to "catch" a husband if she had no sample of her needlework to casually show to a beau. Embroidery "samplers" were religiously worked by young girls from the age of eight to eighteen; "religiously" was an apt description, too, because these samplers almost always included a Bible verse, a prayer, or at least a very obvious moral.

E xperienced needlewomen were said to make nine stitches to an inch when quilting. Some women found it difficult to reach the centre row of the quilt. In such case, a child might be asked to sit beneath the quilting frames and thrust the needle up through the several folds of material to the quilter above, enabling her to finish that last, hard-to-reach row of stitches.

Many old patchwork quilt designs had a special meaning. For instance, the red centre in the Log Cabin design was claimed to represent the fire in the hearth, while the outer strips of material represented the logs - dark strips for the cold northern side of the cabin and brighter strips for the sunny southern exposure. Actually, the pieces of the Log Cabin design were often fitted into many different patterns and did not always include a red centre. In the frugal pioneering days, housewives used whatever they had on hand, and more of the fabric scraps tended to be dull than bright.

A t a time when transportation was slow and much work had to be done outside in the heat of a summer day, protection from the sun was a serious matter. Usually one female member of a family was taught by an older member to fashion hats from available straw.

Strong, straight stalks of wheat straw were gathered individually and soaked in water for several days to increase pliability. Then the straws were woven or plaited into braids about three feet long, and these were carefully stitched together. The crown was shaped first, then the sides and the brim, which was sometimes made so wide that the hat was called an "umbrella hat".

Women and girls also wore cloth sunbonnets, even after the turn of the century.

These usually covered the nape of the neck to prevent sunstroke. In fashionable circles, women carried parasols as well - a custom most impractical for someone working in the fields or garden.

The multitudinous talents of pioneer women often included that of general practitioner. In almost every settled area, one woman became a self-appointed and unanimously acclaimed midwife, to be called upon at a baby's birth. Also, with homesteads miles apart and few doctors available, every housewife was expected to have some knowledge of "simples" and "benefits". "Simples" referred to herbs used for remedial purposes, while "benefits" described the old-fashioned herbs considered beneficial to everyday well-being.

In fact, herbs were so important to the pioneer housewife that they were often planted among tree stumps or in protected corners of a clearing even before the log cabin was completed. Aside from their medicinal value, they were used as flavourings in sometimes not-so-fresh foods, as aromatic mixtures, as preservatives, and as insect repellents.

Horehound was one of the more important remedial herbs, used to combat throat irritations. Combined with other herbs, honey, licorice, or black currants, it fought a bitter battle against colds and whooping cough. It could be made into a form of lozenge, but was more pleasant as horehound candy.

Edna Bryan's Horehound Candy

Steep one teaspoon of dried and ground horehound leaves in one cup of boiling water for two or three hours. Press the leaves occasionally, strain, and pour the liquid into a pot. Add one cup of brown sugar, one cup of white sugar, one-quarter cup of corn syrup, and one-quarter teaspoon of salt. Simmer to dissolve the sugar and boil to 246° (use a candy thermometer if possible), gradually increasing the heat. Add one heaping teaspoon of white sugar. Cook to 310°. Boil to the "hard crack" stage, remove at once, and pour quickly into an 8″ square greased pan. Scrape leftover bits into a separate dish, as they will granulate. Cut the candy before it cools (kitchen shears work well) and set out the pieces on a platter. Use as lozenges or add a piece to a cup of boiling water to sooth an irritated throat.

The old saying "What keeps out the heat, keeps out the cold" was taken seriously by Canadian settlers. Medical books cautioned mothers to always keep wool or flannel against the children's chests, winter or summer. Layers of paper were often worn under coats to protect back and chest during long winter walks or sleigh rides. And soles of paper were frequently fitted inside boots for warmth and comfort.

Chaps and "hacks" (open cuts caused by wind and snow) were a common problem in winter, since people had no alternative but to work and travel in inclement weather.

Pure mutton tallow was considered the very best treatment, because of the lanolin it contained. If someone in the family was threatened with a cold, mustard or red pepper was added to the water in his nightly foot bath. And to a sick child or adult, there was nothing as soothing, satisfying, and nourishing as a "nice bowl of gruel". Gruel was a thin porridge made from oat- or corn-meal, thoroughly cooked, seasoned with sugar and a pinch of salt. Usually it was strained and milk was added. This smooth pick-me-up saw many a family through a siege of winter ailments.

Very simple ingredients were called for in what was referred to as a "celebrated salve":

¼ pound of mutton tallow
¼ pound of beeswax
3 pound of rosin
Combine, melt, then add to cold water. Pull and work in the same way as for "pulled candy" or shoemaker's wax. A cure-all for cuts, old sores, and bruises, and used in "plasters" for pleurisy and rheumatism.

According to the well-known nursery rhyme, when Jack fell down and broke his crown, "He went to bed to mend his head with vinegar and brown paper." While this might not be the accepted treatment for today's tumbler, many of the old-fashioned remedies are still acceptable.

The old people claimed that a person should eat asparagus to purify the blood, celery to cure rheumatism and neuralgia, and lettuce to induce sleep. Chicken fat was said to relieve earache and reduce deafness. The leaves of the common geranium, bruised and applied to a cut, would heal it in no time. White sugar sprinkled on a bad cut, according to one elderly lumberman, stopped profuse bleeding and promoted healing. A spider web spread across a wound was believed to cause the blood to clot. And a handwritten receipt in an old family cookbook reads: "Equal parts of wheat flour and salt will stop bleeding. Bind on with a cloth for man or beast."

Hot water applied for fifteen or twenty minutes at the onset of a cold sore was the only real deterrent. A stye on the eyelid could be removed, it was said, by applying steeped black tea leaves sewn into a small bag. If that didn't work, it could be charmed away by someone repeating three times, "You've a stye on your eye," to which the patient was expected to reply, "It's a lie." Third time's the charm!

Although eventually candles could be bought in town or from a pedlar, most housewives in backwoods settlements and villages found it more practical to make their own, either by dipping or by pouring into moulds. Candle dipping was the cheapest and quickest method of mass-producing everyday candles, which along with the fireplace were the main source of light in early homes. Even so, people lit candles only when it became absolutely necessary, and often "sat the grey remainder of the evening out" as did Andrea del Sarta in Browning's poem.

The two main requisites for homemade candles were candlewick and animal fat. Wicking was "store-boughten" or obtained from the pedlar for a few cents a ball, and was usually purchased in quantity, but the earliest settlers often sent home to the "mother country" for wick.

Since tallow was often scarce, all refuse fat was stored away until there was enough to make candles or soap. In a farming community, tallow from beef or sheep was most easily obtained; if an old ox died, the tallow rendered from it would make upwards of three hundred candles. Pork fat, while available, was too soft to be useful in candlemaking, although it was used extensively in baking, soapmaking, and lard-lamps. In some Canadian communities, moose fat was used a great deal. And strangely enough, bear fat, which was said to have no objectionable odour during the rendering process, was preferred by those who lived in "bear country". All pure tallow candles would eventually become rancid, so honey-fragrant beeswax was added when possible. Enterprising chandlers even added wild ginger or other fragrant substances to counteract the odour of the animal fat.

Tallow was rendered by being melted very slowly in water, perhaps several times, to remove impurities. The water would eventually evaporate and the wax-like liquid could be poured off and carefully strained. Then it was chilled in a clean container until it contracted. At that point it could be lifted out in a white block, ready for use in soap or candles. Tallow rendered in summer tended to be soft and yellow; often it was bleached and firmed by boiling in a solution of alum and hot water for an hour or so.

Dipping candles was a messy chore. If possible, it was done out-of-doors, but when it was necessary to dip indoors, pieces of bark or wood were placed underneath the hanging candles to protect the floor.

The rendered tallow was remelted over fire in a large container partly filled with hot water, which kept it in liquid form. In the meantime, five or six wicks, each about a foot long, were strung on a single dowel or stick. (Double wicks made longer-lasting, brighter flames.) Several "wick'd" dowels were placed crosswise over long rods which rested on the backs of two chairs over the tub of tallow. The wicks were then lowered to become coated with tallow, set aside to cool, another set dipped, and so on. Many dippings were required to bring a candle to usable size, and it was necessary to cool the candles after each dipping. Many of the older women prided themselves on the fine candles they could make by dipping; they straightened each candle before a successive dip until its weight was sufficient to hold it more or less straight.

Candles could not be dipped successfully in hot weather, for they would not cool properly. Sometimes freshly dipped candles were plunged into cold water, but this often caused water to become trapped between the layers of tallow and resulted in sputtering candles. Since tallow burned smokily and swiftly, resourceful housewives sprinkled salt over them or dipped them in sudsy wash water to make them less likely to drip or gutter. Also, candlewick was found to burn brighter and with less guttering if it was first dipped in a solution of lime water and salt petre.

In poorer homes, the finished "tallow dips" were stuck onto a saucer by slightly melting one end, or were jammed into the neck of a bottle. In more affluent homes, they were placed in candleholders fashioned of materials ranging from wood to brass. Water was sometimes placed in the deep nursery candleholders as an extra precaution against sparks.

Candle moulds were cylindrical forms into which liquid tallow or wax was poured. They were made of pewter or tin by a tinsmith, who rolled and soldered each cylinder separately, then soldered it onto a frame that held from two to a hundred or more cylinders.

Of course, these moulds were available at the general store or from the pedlar, but they cost money or barter produce, both of which were scarce, and one or two moulds could make only a few candles at a time. Occasionally, an itinerant candlemaker (chandler) made a call with his horse or mule laden down with clattering moulds, and offered to make a supply of candles for a nominal sum.

In moulding candles, the wicks had to be measured, doubled, and forced through the tip end of the mould, then tied to a dowel at the base, pulled taut, and knotted at the tip. Another method was to thread a single, coarser wick through one cylinder and back down through the next, pulling tautly and securing firmly to the rod or dowel. Candle moulds had to be kept scrupulously clean for easy removal of the candles. A vinegar rinse, after careful washing, rendered the moulds greaseless, so that after the knots were cut the candles could be readily released. Sometimes, especially in cold weather, it was necessary to dip the moulds momentarily in hot water.

Candles made entirely of firm and fragrant beeswax were great favourites. They were difficult to obtain, however, because even the few families who kept bees were often obliged to barter the wax for greater necessities. But when beeswax was available, a few candles would be made in moulds and stored away for special occasions.

In the maritime regions, luxurious candles were made of bayberry and also stored away. They were naturally a pretty green shade and, like beeswax candles, were long-lasting. They were in great demand, too, since a bushel of bayberries made only a few candles. The tiny, radish-like seeds of the bayberry were simmered until the wax floated to the surface and could be strained off.

Soapmaking was another run-of-the-mill chore for early homemakers. The basic recipe varied little; lye and grease were the main ingredients, with borax, ammonia, or rosin sometimes added. For toilet soap, such beauty aids as rolled oats, sugar, or glycerine might be added, and perhaps bergamot, wild ginger leaves, or aromatic sassafras for scent.

Pioneer soapmakers "dripped the lye" by adding rain water to hickory, maple, or other hardwood ashes, which had been placed in a wooden hopper, trough, or half-barrel with a perforated base. This was known as an "ash leach". The liquid was allowed to drain off into an earthenware vessel below, to be added to grease for making soap. Lye provided the cleansing quality and tallow removed the danger from the lye. The same results were later obtained by using "store-boughten" lye crystals, with similar precautions taken.

Simple Soap

Melt five or six pounds of fat in two and one-half pints of soft (rain) water, then set aside. When cool, carefully sprinkle in one can of lye crystals. Stir until cool, as the lye will reheat it, then stir occasionally until it thickens. Pour into a wooden or cardboard box lined with cloth, and score with a knife. Next day, or when completely cold, cut into bars.

To Remember When Making Lye Soap

1. Lye is dangerous; it will burn skin. Wear long sleeves and gloves.
2. Never pour grease *into* lye in a pot. Always add lye to the grease.
3. Use lye when there are no children or pets about.
4. Use earthenware utensils. Iron or stone crock or granite will do, but never galvanized iron or tin - the lye will "eat" through these.
5. Always use a wooden spoon, stick, or paddle.
6. If grease is salty, it should be boiled and skimmed when cool, preferably a day or two previously.
7. Grease should be warm but not hot, and lye should be at room temperature. Lye will heat water, so let it cool.

8. The more the soap is stirred until it begins to thicken, the whiter it will become, and the lighter in weight.
9. A tablespoon or two of oil of sassafras will cut the fatty odour and add fragrance.
10. As with tallow candles, the longer soap is stored before use, the firmer and more long-lasting it will be.

Come Saturday night, in almost every home the bath was a once-a-week ritual. A big tub was set out (before the fireplace or wood stove in winter months), with a good-sized bar of homemade soap near by. A screen, often fashioned of blankets spread over the backs of chairs, kept the heat from escaping and provided privacy for the bather. The children took turns, usually youngest to eldest, or perhaps cleanest to dirtiest, with an extra kettle of hot water added to the tub for each bather. Leisurely winter baths are fictional only; cooling water, cold houses, and lack of privacy prevented them.

Swing Around the Demijohn

"We hung the iron crane to-night,
And merry was the feast and long."

– Henry Wadsworth Longfellow

The farmhouse was the true social centre of early rural Canada, the site of most get-togethers from weddings to funerals. And often the first social event in a new home was the "hanging of the crane"; friends and neighbours would join in the celebration as the crane or trammel (the iron bar from which kettles were hung) was secured in the fireplace. Similar to modern house-warming festivities, this tradition was a formal indication that the couple was "setting up house" permanently.

Communal working "bees", church socials and related events, and an occasional "chivaree", or surprise party following a wedding, were always antici-pated events. Organized gatherings were few and far between, though, and in the meantime people used the slightest excuse for a visit, believing that "the way to a friend's home is never long." Excitement ran high, for instance, when a neighbour brought home his first "store-boughten" coal-oil lamp and was about to light it. The family and visitors stood in awe at a safe distance, and for weeks afterwards neigh-bours left candle-lit homes to view this latest acquisition.

In the more isolated backwoods areas, settlers would often halloo to the nearest neighbour each morning to let him know that all was well. As an answering halloo echoed back, a feeling of well-being was established in an otherwise lonely settlement.

Letter-writing was the accepted means of communication during the nineteenth century. (Although the telephone was invented during the latter half, it did not come into general use until after the turn of the century.) Postage was expensive and was paid at a letter's destination by the recipient. For this reason, a letter was often criss-crossed – that is, written horizontally on the paper and then, after the page had been given a half-turn, written in the space between words.

Many hands make light work" was a well-practiced pioneer maxim; a working "bee" was called for any task from quilting to raising a house or barn. It was considered an honour to be invited to a bee, and an individual would actually feel slighted if left out.

Usually, as the men worked out-of-doors, the women prepared vast quantities of food, chatting all the while. A social hour was often held later in the evening to celebrate the completed task.

In an era when people were almost completely dependant on each other for assistance and fellowship, nothing was considered too good for a neighbour. People gladly worked together, and if a neighbour helped out all day with the threshing or building, it was unthinkable that he would go home to eat. "You eat where you scratch!" was the down-to-earth philosophy of the rural people. If a man were obliged to leave early for any reason, an early supper was prepared for him.

In the days when community life centred around the church, the annual "social" was the event of the year. Women carried food for miles over rough roads, often on foot. "Stump speeches" were delivered, romances bloomed, and lithe youngsters stole away to the old swimming hole, "if one perchance was nigh", for a quick skinny-dip while adults caught up on the news of the community.

A "taffy pull" was a popular entertainment in earlier kitchens, a special treat for a group of children at Christmas gatherings and an accepted pastime for courting couples on a long winter evening. The candy

could be flipped over a hook and pulled by a single person or simply flipped over one hand and then the other, but it was more fun if the taffy were pulled by two people.

Almost every "cookery" book had a "receipt" for taffy, but perhaps the most fascinating one appeared in a late nineteenth-century book by the famous Dr. Chase.

Dr. Chase's Molasses Candy

"Take equal amounts of brown sugar and molasses, and put them into a suitable kettle and when it begins to boil, skim it well, strain it, or else pour it through a fine wire sieve to free it of slivers and sticks which are often found in the sugar, then return it to the kettle and continue to boil, until when you have dipped your hand in cold water and passed one or two fingers through the boiling candy and immediately back to the cold water, what adheres, when cold, will crush like dry egg shells, and does not adhere to the teeth when bitten.

"When done, pour it on a stone or platter which has been greased, and as it cools, begin to throw up the edges and work it by pulling on a hook or by the hand, until bright and glistening like gold (the hands should have a little flour on them occasionally), now keep the mass by a warm stove (if much is made at one time), and draw it into stick size, occasionally rolling them to keep round, until all is pulled out and cold, then with shears, clip a little upon them, at proper lengths for the sticks, and they will snap quickly while yet the stick will bend; no colour, no butter, no lard or flavour is used or need be, yet any oil can be used for flavouring, if desired, when poured out to cool. Sugar left in molasses barrel works very nicely in this preparation. Pulverized white sugar sprinkled amongst it will prevent it from sticking together."

In earlier days, singing and whistling were not reserved for those with formal training only; people did not care if their voices were unequal to that of the primadonna performing at the Old Russell House. They sang simply to express their emotions, while they worked, during slow travel, to pass the time, and for the sheer joy of it. They sang lullabies, love songs, spinning and churning ditties, and hymns around the organ or piano on a Sunday evening – songs that still rouse feelings of old-time togetherness.

A fiddler and a piano player, or perhaps just somebody "good on the mouth organ", could provide all the music required for a good old-fashioned "hoe-down". And there was always someone especially adept at "calling off" for a square dance. Age and energy determined whether a person joined the party or merely tapped his toes and watched as the lamp or candles literally danced on the table.

Of course, dancing was not permitted on the Sabbath, and some religious groups frowned upon dancing any time. But social life often took the form of singing and "swinging 'round the demijohn" (a glass wine jug encased in a straw covering that was too often, and too soon, emptied).

When someone was said to be "spruced up" in olden days, in all probability it meant he had drawn off a little too much spruce beer. This was a favourite beverage, kept in a cask or keg with a handle for easy toting to the fields or woods. If the keg or cask became musky, a little sulphur was burned in it and allowed to stand for a day or two before re-using.

Spruce Beer

Boil well a teaspoon of ginger and an ounce of hops in a gallon of water. Strain and add two cups of molasses and about

62

one-half ounce of essence of spruce (you may boil sprigs of spruce to obtain this essence). Cool and add a teacup of yeast. Allow to ferment for a day or two in a jar, before bottling and sealing.

Dandelion wine occasionally offered another excuse for a little imbibing. Usually, though, it was handed out very sparingly, and then only to special guests or to somebody recovering from an illness, for it was considered a good tonic. As soon as the summer blossoms became plentiful, children throughout the country were swished out the door, armed with bucket or basket, to collect the sunny dandelion blooms.

The Family's Dandelion Wine

Pour one gallon of boiling water over a gallon crock full of dandelion heads. Let stand for a day or overnight. Strain the liquid and grate into it the rinds of three oranges and one lemon; add the orange and lemon juice and boil for fifteen minutes. Add three to four pounds of white sugar and let cool. Spread a slice of toast

with yeast and add. Let stand for three to four weeks or until the end of fermentation. Put in bottles and cork.

Swing around, swing around, swing around the demijohn, Swing the pretty girl around the demi, demijohn!" So went the old song, as the jugs of wine were emptied. In the days when homebrew was a handy thirst-quencher, drunkenness caused untold misery. Drinking was indulged in by the men only in most homes, and was usually heartily frowned upon by the women – in fact, often the men hid their liquor in a hay mow or loft, except upon a really social occasion. But even in the home of the so-called abstainer liquor was sometimes taken under the guise of medicine; and, of course, it often was medicine.

Drunkenness became so widespread by the nineteenth century that the Church of England issued a booklet of non-alcoholic beverage recipes, including instructions for such drinks as raspberry vinegar, lemon drinks, rhubarb juice, and a simple drink of raw oatmeal and water, stirred well, that was a favourite with Scottish people.

Temperance societies were formed, temperance songs were sung; yet despite such heartrending wailings as "Father, oh Father, come home with me now" and "My father was a drunkard, my mother, she is dead", the demijohn remained much in evidence in many homes.

A chew of tobacco, the older men maintained, was a sure-fire prevention against a dust-filled throat at a harvest or threshing bee, and there was certain to be at least one of them with a "plug" to pass around. In this way, young men were often initiated into the questionable joys of chewing tobacco. Bitter and hot with a hint of molasses taste, it was said to be a real test to separate the men from the boys.

And children were not without "chewing gum" in days of yore. A type of gum could be made from melted paraffin, a little olive oil, and glycerine, to which a drop or two of flavouring was added. Clean wheat, chewed for a few minutes, also became a delightful elastic-like gum – and was nutritious, too. Fresh wax from the honey comb was also pleasant chewing.

Spruce gum, straight from the tree, was popular with pioneer children and adults alike, as well as with many of their descendants. In fact, the harvesting of spruce gum became a quite lucrative industry in the Maritimes when the gum was sold commercially.

There was never a need for trained child-care workers in earlier years, to concoct fun and games for the young. Children had imaginations and were very well told to use them. A swing, they knew, need not be a seat hung between two ropes and attached to a crossbar above. It could be a young girl's sturdy skirt flipped up over a post so that she could lean back and sway. A "happy tree" hanging across a brook also made an exciting swing. Usually the children clambered up the trunk of the tree on one side of the creek and daringly worked their way down the overhanging branches swinging to the ground on the other side. Besides being fun, it resulted in better co-ordination and muscle control than many later organized athletics.

Another favourite summer pastime - and another test for children's wear of yesterday - involved turning the bank of the creek into an otter slide by splashing a few buckets of water onto it. After an uproarious hour or two on the splash slide, they "washed" their clothing while wearing it, by using the white clay "soap" from the bank opposite and rinsing in the old swimming hole before the homeward trek.

Ball was often played with a pig bladder that had been washed and dried and perhaps stuffed. "Auntie-I-Over" consisted of simply tossing a "store-boughten" ball over a rooftop to the catcher on the other side, with, of course, the accompanying shout. Hide-and-seek or stoop-tag might go on for hours. A see-saw could be made by balancing a plank over an old saw-horse. Hopscotch and "Mother May I" were popular pastimes, and so was "dressing up" in costumes from an old trunk. Hoop rolling was also popular; on village streets and country lanes, children rolled hoops from barrels or kegs, iron buggy tires, or wooden hoops specially "turned" for the purpose, with the aid of a small straight stick or a long stick with a short crossbar. Chasing June beetles at twilight and fire flies after dark were great sleep-inducers, if such a thing were needed!

Winter sports were almost as many and varied as those of summer. Building snow forts, indulging in snowball battles, sliding down snow-clad hills with or without a sleigh or toboggan, and even just sliding along on foot over a patch of ice were all great fun. There was skating on the pond too, of course, after having learned by pushing a chair about, and ice sailing and snow shoeing.

One exciting though dangerous sport was to tie a sled or toboggan behind a fast sleigh and be towed for miles. It was not uncommon in some areas to see the family dog or perhaps a goat or sheep hitched to a makeshift sled or toboggan. Children also took turns pulling each other on the iron-runnered sleighs, which were not made for deep snow but were great for "belly whackers" on a well-packed hill.

Indoor winter fun included "Upset the Fruit Basket", taffy pulls, sing-songs, music, or step-dancing, and whittling for the boys and needlework or even elocution for the girls. Tea-tray tobogganing down the stairs became a fashionable sport in many of the well-to-do homes in the late nineteenth century, even for young adults. As with most sports, it sometimes proved dangerous. Sliding downstairs in clean bran sacks was also fun, if a little bumpy, and of course there was always the banister for a speedy descent.

Some children's games and pastimes centred around buttons, which were an important addition to clothing during the nineteenth century. "Button, button, who's got the button?" was a favourite game when little ones got together at Christmas, or for small children in a big family. A string of buttons down a dress was quite a challenge to the girls, who "read" them one by one, chanting "Tinker, tailor, soldier, sailor . . ." to determine who they would marry.

Button collecting became quite a popular hobby, especially with young girls, who began their collections with a special, large, colourful button known as a "touch" button which they would thread on a "charm string". According to one legend, when the goal of a thousand buttons was reached, a wish on the touch button would supposedly bring a girl's dream prince. Another version claimed that the 999th was the lucky button, and to add the 1000th would doom the collector to spinsterhood.

In either case, imagine the hours spent counting hundreds of buttons hundreds of times, in the belief that a single button could mean the difference between a blissful marriage and a life of "single blessedness".

Even a century ago, each spring a young man's fancy turned to "thoughts of love", and the girl he seriously courted was often no older than "sweet sixteen".

The aim of all young girls was to grow a "crowning glory" of hair long enough to sit on. By the time they had accomplished this, they were usually young ladies, and the fashion for demure young ladies was to

"put up" their hair. They used strips of rags or twisted paper to curl their hair during the night, and old-time curling irons or tongs, heated over a fire, candle, or lamp, for last-minute or emergency curling. Matrons with long hair were said to carry as much as forty or fifty miles of hair on their heads; it would keep on growing and was seldom cut. Some with skimpy hair wore wigs or "switches", but few would admit to this vanity.

The special vanity of men was a beard and full head of hair. Macassar oil, a favourite hairdressing, was made by combining a quart of olive oil, two and one-half ounces of alcohol, one-half dram of rose oil, and an ounce of alkanet root tied in muslin bags until it turned a red colour. The bag was then hung so the oil could drain from it, to be collected in a jar or bottle and applied on special occasions. This oil posed a problem to the lady of the house, though, who resorted to crocheting doilies known as anti-macassers to place on the back of the gentlemen's parlour chairs.

Choose your bride on a Saturday, not on a Sunday" was the advice once given to eligible young men, who tended to be attracted to frills. But practicality was a must in those days, and very often a bride was chosen with her culinary accomplishments in mind. A suitor was quick to notice if her bake-board or dough box were scraped too clean, denoting meanness, or if it were left too floury, suggesting that she would be a spendthrift and a sloppy housekeeper.

More romances began at funerals than at weddings then, too. A young woman's real worth became evident at a funeral - not only her kindness and sympathy but her ability to "feed the multitudes". After all, relatives and friends who had travelled long distances had to be "put up" - and put up with - perhaps for days.

And, understandably, marriages of convenience were common in those days. Often, a sudden death left young children motherless; or sometimes a widow had no alternative but to remarry to keep a roof over the heads of her children.

Spooning" was an old expression that came to mean courting. It originated from a custom in which a young hopeful bestowed the gift of a spoon on a belle to let her know his intentions. In some of the stricter families, after a few calls the young man might be asked by the girl's parents if his intentions were honourable and perhaps even if he were prepared to support her "in the manner to which she was accustomed".

For the sake of propriety, a single girl of marriageable age was expected to always be accompanied by an older, married woman, even when being courted. The ordeal of a formal proposal was also considered proper form, as was the young lady's deferment to "think it over". For the suitor, the proposal was equalled only by the trauma of confronting a stern papa to ask for his daughter's hand in marriage.

A long engagement usually followed (except in the case of shotgun weddings and marriages of convenience), during which time the practical bride filled a hope chest to overflowing with linen and lace and finely stitched quilts. A bride was expected to have thirteen quilts packed in her pine chest as part of her dowry (although thirteen was not usually a "lucky" number; it was considered very unlucky, for example, to seat thirteen persons at a table for a meal). The thirteenth quilt was often quilted only after the young lady's wedding plans were made public.

Also, according to an unwritten rule, a betrothed young lady was, in plain terms, supposed to "have her teeth fixed". Apparently the idea was that she would bear a child every two years (if she nursed her babies in between), and "for every child a mother would lose a tooth", because a child was thought to take the calcium from the mother.

A wedding couple in olden days almost always posed for a photograph with the man seated and his bride standing behind him, typically, ready to serve. And if the subjects give the impression that they were wired in place, in fact they were. Such was the mechanism of the early cameras that it was necessary to remain perfectly still for as long as an hour.

Children born to parents several generations ago often had "virtuous" names bestowed upon them. Such names as Faith, Patience, Hope, Prudence, and Charity were common. Also, biblical names were frequently used - John, Noah, Mary, Elizabeth, Benjamin, Sarah, Daniel, Luke, Joseph, Matthew, and Abraham. Most babies were also "called after" a member of the family, and people in the family or community with similar names were identified by adjectives, such as Big John, Red Luke, Lame William, Cousin Hannah, Smiling Joe, Lucky Thomas, Charlie Look-up, Spittin' Jim, Long Alec, Stutterin' Sam, or even Yawning Jack.

Of course, hard feelings were occasionally caused by indiscreet choosing of an infant's name. Sometimes an extra name was hurriedly added to assuage the injured pride of a relative or friend, especially if he were rich or influential, or if he were living in the same house as the parents.

In days when two or three generations were often obliged to live in close quarters in the same home, family squabbles were common. While it may have been "character-building" for children to live with aunts or grandpa's cousin Jane or Uncle Joe, as well as with their parents, it could be a strain on everyone involved. In fact, it was not uncommon for people living in the same house to go without speaking directly to each other for years. They often resorted to indirect communication, known as "talking through the cat".

On the whole, though, when two or three generations shared a home, children seemed to have a better understanding of life and death. And the older people had an honoured and responsible position in the family; it was they who were familiar with the remedies, lore, and recipes, and it was they who handed down this wealth of knowledge, mostly verbally, to the following generation.

Shank's Mare

"Never any weary traveller complained
That he came too soon to his journey's end."

- Thomas Fuller

Hardship and heartbreak faced prospective settlers even before they reached Canada's shores. Those from "the homeland" soon learned that weeks of ocean travel meant illness, misery, a woeful lack of privacy, and a great deal of thieving aboard ship. Many families concealed their "treasures" in secret compartments built into the old wooden chests they brought with them; but in some cases the entire chest was stolen upon embarkation, even by a person paid to deliver it. Death aboard ship was not uncommon, and since burial at sea seemed heartless, especially if a child had died, bodies were occasionally smuggled ashore for "proper" burial.

Upon arrival in Canada, settlers faced further suffering and despair, trudging across a strange, wooded land on foot or bumping over rough oxen trails. Roads in early Canada were little more than paths through the woods and swamps. Except in very high country, they were almost always wet and soggy, and often impassable. Many settlers acquired ox-drawn carts for hauling their possessions, but the wheels would often sink axle-deep in the water and mud, and the men and sometimes the women would exert all their strength to extricate them.

Waterways were the only smooth highways for summer or winter travel. But even these highways were by no means accident-free. Rapids, violent storms, and, during early winter and early spring, the deceptive snow-covered thin ice caused countless mishaps and occasionally death.

Inland homes and out-buildings were usually built in the centre of the property so the hauls would be shorter at harvest-time. This resulted in long lanes that were forced to wind around immovable trees and rocks. Although this seemed practical in days when oxen and horses were the main means of transportation, with the advent of motor vehicles in later years these long winding lanes created maintenance problems.

Many other settlers chose sites by rivers or lakes to make use of water transportation, but these farms sometimes were less fertile than the inland bush-lots which had nurtured towering trees. In many sections, too, the settlers had asked friends to procure acreage for them prior to their arrival, or else were expected to simply "draw lots" for land, often with disappointing results. Later settlers who were fortunate enough to live near "parts" where the railroad passed through found themselves with a high and dry road for walking to town.

In the days of poor roads and few horses, the main means of transportation was "by shank's mare" - in other words, walking. People were obliged to walk for miles, even in their "good clothes", and they often took shortcuts between two points or across a neighbour's property. At places where they most frequently crossed over a fence, stiles were built; these were stairs constructed on either side of the fence, with a single plank landing on top to facilitate crossing. A stile was a great clothes-saver, protecting clothing from brambles and rough logs. And since clambering over a high log fence would pose a real problem in an era when it was considered immodest for a lady to "show her ankles", a stile afforded a less awkward crossing. Most farm animals, though, like the pig in the old nursery rhyme, "would not go over the stile".

Accidents in the woods, on the river, and over the uncertain roads during inclement weather were only too common. A fall from a "spooked" horse, for example, or a runaway team could result in serious injury. Even becoming lost in the woods might be fatal; children sent out to pick berries or bring in the cattle easily lost their bearings, and old people frequently wandered off aimlessly, and were not always able to find the way back home.

It was not unusual for a traveller to be wounded by a wild animal, or gored, sometimes fatally, by an angry bull. In countries "infested with wolves", travellers were advised to carry along some sort of musical instrument to play enroute; the noise was said to work on the animal's nerves, causing it to halt and howl, during which time the traveller could escape to a safe distance. And of course, if someone had to camp in the woods for the night, a fire was considered a good deterrent against wild animals.

The milk maid, safe through driving rains and snows, / Wrapped in her cloak and propp'd on pattens, goes," wrote Soame Jenyns in the mid eighteenth century. Pattens were raised wooden (or later, steel) shoes, onto which regular shoes or boots were attached, for walking over wet or muddy surfaces in the days when these conditions existed in many areas.

Covered bridges were never plentiful in Ontario, although Quebec and New Bruns-

wick could each boast of more than one thousand in the nineteenth century. Bridges were covered, not to protect the traveller (although they did provide temporary shelter from a storm), but to protect the floorboards and beams of the bridge from the ravages of time and weather. In fact, in winter, travellers often had to shovel snow under the runners of heavily laden sleighs to enable them to pass through the bridge. The inside walls offered convenient advertising space for merchants who wished to extoll the virtues of their products to journeymen, local farmers, and housewives. Covered bridges were sometimes referred to as "kissing bridges", perhaps because they were popular sites for rendezvous.

Originally, most covered bridges were privately built and maintained, but as traffic became heavier, many were converted to toll bridges to help finance repairs needed because of weathering and flooding. Toll gates, posting amounts required for the passing through of vehicles and stock, were erected at the entrance.

Toll gates were a nuisance as well as an expense to penny-pinching pioneers. These were placed at the more frequently travelled crossroads, and the house of the toll-gate keeper often had a large window so that a "sharp eye could be kept out" for travellers.

Some travellers would go many miles out of their way to avoid paying a toll. To the more adventurous, however, it became a daring game to "bilk the toll" – that is, to race the horses through before the toll-gate keeper realized what was happening. A famous mid nineteenth-century painting by Cornelius Kreighoff depicts a sleigh full of adventurers "cheating the toll" or "running the toll gate"; and a Currier and Ives painting of the same decade shows a "crash team" galloping headlong through the wooden gate.

Half-way houses sprang up in earlier years in many sections of Canada. These inns were usually built thirty-five or forty miles apart, the distance a stage coach could travel during the course of a day over hazardous roads. Such accommodation was often "rough" but not always "ready", for a sudden blizzard might fill the inn to overflowing. In that case, it is said, extra mattresses were simply thrown on the floor.

Usually a bar offered liquid refreshment to gentlemen travellers, but the ladies and children were expected to sit sedately with their needlework in the ladies' sitting room

until dinner was announced. At that time, they hoped to be joined by the gentlemen.

Privacy was lacking in most half-way houses, and conditions were often unsanitary. Cuspidors, commonly known as "spittoons", were greatly in evidence but often ignored. In fact, according to one oft-told story, an inkeeper one day asked his wife where his spittoon had disappeared to. "I've missed it!" he exclaimed. "That's why it disappeared," she curtly replied.

The early one-horse carts, the stage coach, and the later buggies and "rigs" were built with high wheels, for easier travel over rough, usually muddy roads. "The higher the wheel, the easier to pull," went the old saying. Low-wheeled vehicles were said to "pull a horse heavier", and many horses were literally worked to death in the days before the "horseless carriage" came into general use.

Considering the climate and road conditions in most sections of early Canada, illustrations depicting the "coach and four" dainty horses are certainly erroneous. Horses of sturdy build and even temperament were called for. During the days when the "horse and rig" was the accepted mode of transportation, horses received much the same treatment automobiles do today. A careful, considerate horseman would have a road-worthy "roadster" for a much longer time than would his reckless neighbour.

Pedlar and the Emporium

"If there were dreams to sell,
What would you buy?"

– Thomas Lovell Beddoes

Prior to the establishment of the country general store, and even afterwards, itinerant salesmen spread out from the towns to peddle their goods throughout the countryside. It has been said that a pedlar would not hesitate to sell even his "horse and rig" if he thought he could gain by such a transaction.

The pedlar's call was an exciting event, for children especially, as boxes, bags, and chests were opened to reveal all sorts of fascinating necessities and luxuries. Household articles, beauty aids, candle-wicking, and pots and pans could be bought for a few pennies, but in the average home pennies were hard to come by.

Itinerant" described anyone who travelled from place to place, plying his trade and staying with different families for a week or a fortnight. Sometimes referred to as "journeymen", salesmen of all descriptions, pedlars, and even saddle-back preachers travelled throughout the countryside in search of trade or followers. They also carried messages, packages, and gossip from one home to another.

Most tradesmen and artisans were originally itinerant. Doctors, although usually they had an office of sorts in town, were expected to travel under often almost impossible weather and road conditions to visit their patients. Women also travelled to the more affluent homes as dressmakers; they might stay for as long as a month, outfitting the entire family for the season or perhaps even for the year. Women also gave music, singing, and dancing lessons to children in the more prosperous homes, no doubt properly chaperoned.

"Drumming up business" was an expression used with regard to itinerants. Drums, loud music of some sort, bells, singing, or a "barker" call accompanied their rigs - anything to gain attention and attract a crowd large enough to merit "setting up shop" temporarily.

The ragpicker with his old horse and cart travelled through the streets of villages and towns and out onto the country roads, announcing his approach by droning his request for discards: "Any raaaaaaags? Any booooooones? Any booooooottles today?" The rough old collector no doubt wore many of the rags he acquired from the households along the way. And in later years he asked for feathers, too, especially as feather ticks went out of vogue and were being discarded or sold for next to nothing.

Although people today may feel they have invented the idea of recycling, the ragpicker of yesterday turned the rags over to the printer to be made into paper (cloth still makes the best paper), or to the weaver to be converted into rag rugs. The bones he collected were used for fertilizer, glue, and such, and the bottles were returned to be refilled.

Since money was scarce in those days, the barter system was commonly used, and most household needs were acquired through trade. The farmer's wife exchanged dairy produce for other practical needs at the general store, the carpenter might build furniture for the bootmaker to pay for his family's footwear, and the cooper would provide a tub for the broom-maker in exchange for a good corn broom.

The first shop of the early artisan or craftsman was usually in his home; customers entered by the "shop door", while friends and relatives used the private family entrance. Later, as the tradesman's business expanded, a shop was built near by (in the same way that the other settlers built a second home), providing extra living quarters for his family.

Originally, the blacksmith wrought iron pots and pans and fireplace utensils, as well as forging wheels for all types of old-fashioned vehicles. Eventually a wheelwright took over some of this business, and the blacksmith was gradually called upon to fashion shoes for oxen and horses. When horses and oxen were used only for bush work, shoeing was not necessary, but as roads became more solid and coach or road horses were used more frequently, having the animals "shod" periodically was necessary.

In some remote areas, the blacksmith was the only person who possessed tools suitable for the extraction of teeth. He was also called upon to "bleed" patients, both human and beast (but using different instruments, we presume), in accordance with the idea that diseased blood should be removed for complete recovery. Even after the turn of the century, graduates of veterinary colleges still advertised as being capable of "treating all diseases of the ox, horse, and domestic animal. Dentistry a specialty."

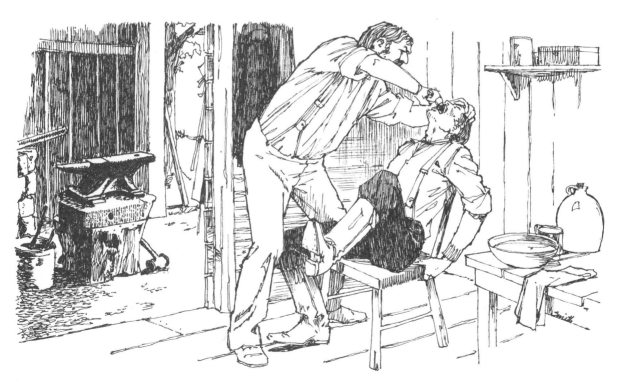

In the days before trade schools, a boy in his early teens would learn his chosen trade by "serving an apprentice" under a blacksmith, shoemaker, harness maker, or other tradesman. Living in his master's home, the poor young apprentice was obliged to perform the menial tasks about the home and shop, and often slept in the loft or attic in the cold of winter or the heat of summer. His apprenticeship usually lasted seven years, after which time he was considered capable of becoming an itinerant tradesman with the prospect of eventually owning a shop of his own.

Most of the old folks continued to conceal their money in the chimney corner, or under the mattress or sewn into it, even after banks had come into general use in the towns. While travelling from market, women often stuffed their hard-earned money down the front of their dresses, "in their bosoms". The high boots worn by the men were also convenient and safe for the purpose of carrying cash.

During the Victorian era, the country general store was often given the glamourized name of emporium. Here the settlers exchanged their farm produce for yearned-for items such as English china, cloth, lace, and at Christmas season perhaps such luxuries as imported oranges and "store-boughten" candies.

Barrels containing brown sugar (often "hard as your boot"), molasses, rendered tallow, and other necessities stood on the floor of the general store.

Almost always the emporium included the post office wicket. Equally important, however, was its value as a quiet social centre, where a game of checkers could be played across a barrel top, and community news and gossip were exchanged. During winter, the pot-bellied stove was always circled by old-timers, warming their feet and airing their views.

Schoolbells and Church Spires

'"Tis education forms the common mind:
Just as the twig is bent the tree's inclined."

– Alexander Pope

The first schools in the early settlements were often informal gatherings of neighbour children at the home of one of the more genteel women of the community. In some areas, more formal classes were held in the home of the schoolmaster.

Eventually, one-room schools of log were built in the more central areas.

Almost always it was a man who took on the chore of teaching. If he came from outside the community, he would live with the different families in turn. Travelling conditions were rough, and quite often so were the pupils, who might be older and bigger than the teacher. He was, out of necessity, a strict disciplinarian.

The formal schoolteacher was very carefully "screened". He must prove himself to be industrious, dedicated, diligent, a non-smoker, frugal, a tee-totaller, and even adept at fashioning quill pens to the taste of the individual pupil. If unmarried, he was permitted one evening for courting, and he was expected to be seen regularly in church on the Sabbath.

In short, he must be of exemplary character. Any swerving from the straight and narrow path would warrant public criticism and possible dismissal. In fact, a story is told in the Ottawa Valley of a young

schoolmaster in the mid nineteenth century who predicted that one day carriages would be driven without horses. The trustees, upon hearing this, made a call to his home and warned him against teaching such heresy.

Each child brought his lunch to school in a pail or basket, and noon hour or recess was often spent filling wood-boxes or fetching water for the teacher. To attend school at all was a gruelling experience, but it was especially so in winter, when it perhaps entailed a trek through snowy bush trails, and also in spring, when it might mean crossing through swamps or over swollen creeks during the spring run-off.

In later years, an old flat-backed horse often carried two or three small children to school - a much safer, drier, and less rugged means of travel. As vehicles became available, roads improved, and the children grew older and more responsible, and if distance merited it, a family might entrust them with a horse and rig or sleigh. "Shank's mare", however, was their usual mode of travel.

The one-room school housed pupils of all ages within its rough interior. Because boys could be spared from home only during the winter months, they were often "big chunks of lads in long trousers" before they had finished their book learning. Understandably, they received a skimpy formal education, extending no further than the rudiments of reading, writing, and arithmetic, and seldom could anyone afford to go on to higher education.

And while young men received what education they could in the one-room schools, undoubtedly the general feeling was that woman's place was in the home; to prepare herself for this was a more essential facet of a young girl's education.

Slates and slate pencils were commonly used in early schools, and in most cases the first teacher to come into a settlement was expected to make his own blackboard. According to an old recipe, liquid slating for blackboards could be made by mixing together 12 drachms of lampblack, 20 drachms of ultramarine blue, 4 ounces of powdered rotton stone, 6 ounces of powdered pumice stone, 8 ounces of shellac, and 4 pints of alcohol. In later years, a prepared blackboard paint became available at the general store.

Books and other academic supplies had to be purchased by the parents. Pupils of the same family were often permitted to sit together at the early double desks so that they might share these luxury items.

While studying their lessons, the children droned audibly and constantly, like a hive of bees. With all classes from the primer to the "continuation class" (comparable to the first year of high school) sharing the same room, the older pupils often acted as teacher's helpers and "heard" the lessons of the younger children.

Reading lessons, especially for the junior classes, were chock-full of obvious morals, which surely did them no harm. What probably did have an adverse effect on them was the morbid choice of reading material. They droned despairingly through such tales and poems as "How I turned the Grindstone" and "Hannah Binding Shoes":

Poor lone Hannah,
Sitting at the window binding shoes,
Faded, wrinkled,
Sitting, stitching, in a mournful muse.

Spelling bees added a light touch. Sides were chosen by two "captains"; and words, simple ones at first and then more difficult ones, were given out by the schoolmaster. Not only was a spelling bee a special treat, but it encouraged competition, which in turn encouraged a good deal of study. Quite often it was a community affair to which other members of the family were invited to attend, and sometimes to participate in.

Chronically ill and crippled children were in greater number in earlier days, and in most cases this meant no formal schooling. Yet while their illiteracy was a common drawback, these people were not necessarily uncouth. Individuals lacking the opportunity to attend school in their younger days acquired an informal education and a certain refinement through their affiliation with the church, the centre of community life.

At first, church services were held in private homes, whenever an itinerant clergyman spent a few days in a new settlement baptizing children, performing marriages, and celebrating communion or mass. Eventually, during the visit of a "circuit rider" clergyman, two services were held at the church or meeting house on Sunday, and people who had travelled for miles brought lunches and spent the day visiting with their friends between services. In the absence of minister or priest, a neighbour or even a member of the family would conduct funeral services.

A clergyman residing in a community was paid in hand-outs of produce and was frequently obliged to take on extra work to eke out an existence. Often, he was expected to serve as schoolmaster and general practitioner, too, if neither of these was available to the congregation or to the community.

Until a roughly hewn church could be built (with adjacent cemetery ground, in most cases) on property donated by a concerned member of the congregation, the schoolhouse doubled as a meeting house.

The old-time church was a cold, cheerless building which the pastor kept warm by delivering a fire-and-brimstone sermon that lasted for at least an hour. Foot warmers were used in the cold pews. Box stoves were installed in the churches when they became available, and the members of the congregation sitting near these were expected to replenish the fire during the service.

A long pole with a "pittance pouch" or a wooden collection box or basket secured on the end was passed into the pews to receive the meagre collection.

Church choirs consisted not of professional singers, but of enthusiastic worshippers, who were led by a willing member with the aid of a tuning fork in the days before an organ or piano was a standard church furnishing.

Our pioneer ancestors relied to a great extent on their spiritual faith; without it, many of them could not have perservered. Bone-weary from toiling in the sun and rain to plant, tend, and harvest crops, with genuine fervour they "raised the song of harvest home". The nineteenth-century hymns of thanksgiving all described their true feelings of gratitude and helped to meet their spiritual needs - Henry Alford's "Come, ye thankful people, come", Anna Coghill's "Work for the night is coming", and the old favourite, "Bringing in the Sheaves":

> By and by the harvest,
> And the labour ended,
> We shall come rejoicing
> Bringing in the sheaves.

"Abide with me" was usually reserved for funeral services, common in the years when people simply "sickened and died" or "became comsumptive" for want of proper food and medical care.

Letter Edged in Black

"The soul would have no rainbow
Had the eyes no tears."
– John Vance Cheney

Yesterday's invalids were always cared for in the home, and there were many more invalids and semi-invalids then than we have today. Hospitals were still in their infancy; because they were used only as a last resort, people came to associate them, not with recovery, but with death. Often, too, operations were not successful, so many people would rather suffer ill-health than risk going "under the knife".

When a chronically ill person was seen "picking the quilts" absent-mindedly with the tips of his fingers, it was a certain sign he was "not long for this world". And if it became evident that an old person was about to "die of natural decay", the family would often take him out into the garden or on the verandah or lawn for a photograph, "just in case". The idea alone, no doubt, would be sufficient cause for a "turn for the worse".

Fascinating tales are told of death-bed promises, hastily given by grief-stricken family members who were later to be consumed by regret, misery, and often guilt.

Swear-on-the-Bible promises, selfishly extracted by the dying person, often concerned love and marriage. Between a betrothed couple, it might be a pledge to never love another; between a bigoted parent and a child, it might be to not marry "out of the faith"; or, in the case of a widow or widower, it might be a promise to not remarry.

Pacts were also made to not forsake an aging parent or a younger brother or sister, and even, upon occasion, to guard the family "skeletons in the closet".

Superstitions concerning death were common. In a few homes, the coffin was handed out through the window because some people felt that it was unlucky to use the door for such a purpose. A person who moved the lamp or candle in the "corpse room" would be "next to go", and one death in a community meant two more to follow.

"Dream of the dead, lose one of the living," people used to say. A bird flying through an open window or fluttering outside a closed window meant news of a death, as did a dog howling during the night. And at the moment of death, some believed, a window should be opened to release the soul.

At the time of death, a crisp strip of black wool, silk, or cotton was hung on the outside of a door as a symbol of mourning within the home. This "crepe on the door" evolved from earlier times in Europe, when a tablet of wood or stone, or a frame bearing the heraldic arms of a deceased person, was placed in front of a house, over a tomb, on a hearse, or in a church.

Telegrams were seldom sent except as a notification of a family death; the delivery of a telegram was therefore cause for great alarm. More commonly, though, a "letter edged in black" was sent, and it was with trembling hands that one was opened.

The dead were laid out by an older, dignified member of the community. This task was performed with all due respect and propriety, and with no thought of reimbursement.

Much stress was placed on the reverence and silence with which this "last labour of love" was accomplished. The body was bathed unobtrusively under a sheet, securely bound with strong fabric, and white socks were placed on the feet. The eyelids were closed by placing wet pads of wool or linen, or even pennies, over them, and the limbs were straightened and the arms folded across the chest. Since embalming was not practiced, in summer it was necessary to set buckets or tubs of ice underneath the casket, which was placed on a table or across two benches.

Coffins of years gone by were built according to the stature of the deceased; in fact, front doors of the homes were usually built larger than the side or back doors, not to impress anyone, but to enable a larger coffin to pass through. Sometimes, to lessen the worry of the bereaved, coffins were built by the man of the house while he was in good health.

The coffin was simply hoisted onto the shoulders of four or six men for carrying to the "burying grounds", or else placed on a wagon if oxen or horses were to be had. In later years, a black hearse, often called the Black Maria, was drawn by coal-black horses, followed by a solemn procession of people walking or riding in horse-drawn vehicles.

Nothing short of personal illness would prevent a man from offering to dig his neighbour's grave. Indeed, he simply showed up, armed with pick and shovel, prepared to perform this last solemn task for his old neighbour.

A year of mourning was strictly adhered to in the early days in Canada. For the first six months after the death of an immediate member of the family, unrelieved black was worn; then this was lessened gradually by adding a white collar or changing to a grey costume. On "deep mourning attire" (called "widow's weeds" in the case of a husband's death) even the buttons were black; after about six months the women in "half mourning" permitted herself to wear grey buttons.

Bereavement was taken more seriously in those days when families and neighbours were closer, not always in miles but certainly in spirit. Bereavement was widespread, too, for diptheria, smallpox, and consumption were common killers. Entire families might be wiped out; in fact, parents often spoke about their "second" family. It was quite common for a man to outlive two or even three wives, for childbearing and constant back-breaking work took their toll. For pioneer women, especially, there was a good deal of truth in the old saying, "Early wed, early dead."

Conclusion

Abide with me . . . " The organ music swelled, and drifted out across the wind-swept hill. The tall, brown, pretentious blocks of stone and marble told of lives filled with hardship; the slender slabs of white, of lives scarce begun, too soon cut off for lack of medical skill.

"Fast falls the eventide . . . " We were gathered for a memorial service in this old cemetery, and as we sang, the figures of the past seemed to rise beyond the stones – the modest as well as the ostentatious, and some unmarked, unknown to us now.

"The darkness deepens . . . " Swiftly they marched by, and proudly. The men tall and darkly dressed – farmers and statesmen, soldiers from the wars, the village black-smith, the keeper of the store, millers, cobblers, stern "men of the cloth", postmaster, teacher, station agent. Full-skirted women, too, in modest garb, their beribboned bonnets pretty but subdued to befit their day.

"Oh, Lord, with me abide . . . " Our voices rose; the wind-swept hill grew empty of all save the gravestones and the well-kept plots, now bright with flowers, and the modern choir and congregation which had come to mourn the dead and honour them.

"Now let us pray . . . " The fragrant air was filled with the spirit of our ancestors; in awe and reverence, with tear-filled eyes, we bowed our heads.